VOGUE KNITTING
TEEN KNITS

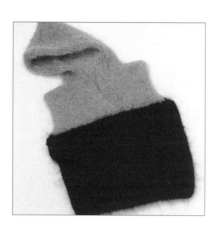

VOGUE KNITTING
TEEN KNITS

SOHO PUBLISHING COMPANY
NEW YORK

SOHO PUBLISHING COMPANY
233 Spring Street
New York, New York 10013

Library of Congress Cataloging-in-Publication Data

Vogue knitting teen knits / [Trisha Malcolm, editor].
p. cm. -- (Vogue knitting on the go!)
ISBN 1-931543-09-7
1. Knitting--Patterns. I. Malcolm, Trisha, 1960- II. Vogue. III. Series.

TT820 .V6255 2003
746.46'20432--dc21   2001049631

Manufactured in China

1 3 5 7 9 10 8 6 4 2

First Edition

TABLE OF CONTENTS

INTRODUCTION

When a teenager enters your life, time takes on a whole new dimension—and there is never enough of it. Teenage years are filled with activity, and you may find that those precious spare minutes you thought you had after work or in the evenings have been instantly devoured by trips to football practice, dress rehearsal, get-togethers with friends, and more. It's exhausting, but even more so for the teen, who, in the process of scrambling to fit it all in, is also learning who he or she is—and expressing that in any way possible.

The sweaters, cardigans, and delightful accessories in this book have been designed with a keen eye on what it means to be a teen—and how an age group that spans only a few years can include such an enormous variety of personalities and tastes. From funky to feminine, bold to basic, these designs have risen to the challenge of providing something to suit every teen's style. But they don't stop there. Each pattern offers a starting point from which you can let your imagination—and your teen's—run wild. Experiment with yarns, colors, stitch patterns, shapes, and lengths until you create the piece that is as one-of-a-kind as your teen.

Let your imagination also help you find those spaces in your schedule—no matter how small—into which you can slip a few stitches. Bring your knitting to her volleyball game or his band concert, purl a row while waiting your turn on the phone, or concoct a cap as you "wait up" after a date. And as you do, take some time to breathe deeply, relax, and marvel at the incredibly unique person your teen is coming to be.

Things are moving fast—including your teen—so grab your needles as you head out the door and get ready to **KNIT ON THE GO!**

THE BASICS

An informal poll was taken among the people who make up the creative and editorial team at Vogue Knitting and we turned up the following result—we all got hooked on knitting as teens. While most of us actually learned to knit at much younger ages, it was in the teen years that we found our true passion for knitting.

Knitting is a rewarding outlet for self-expression and offers endless opportunities for experimentation. With the mind-boggling selection of fibers—linen, silk, mohair, cashmere, cotton, wool, and blends—in hand-dyes, vegetable-dyes, hand-painted palettes, there are so many options today for the creative knitter, both teen and older. Selection of yarns, arrangement of stitches, and placement of motifs reflect your unique perspective on design and style. Knitting, especially quick-knit projects, allows experimenting and the ability to complete a project in no time, a one-of-a-kind creation setting you apart from the crowd.

Collected here are sweaters and accessories meant to appeal to a very broad group of teenagers. Each project requires minimum finishing and is designed to put new skills into practice while building on skills already learned. Your teens may just enjoy knitting the basics themselves—a scarf, hat, mittens, or a sweater—or want someone to create fashion for them. So share your love of this beloved craft with other knitting enthusiasts and call some friends over. Break out your needles and yarn, put out the snacks, and create or recreate some of the most memorable times of your teen years.

SIZING

Since clothing measurements have changed in recent decades, it is important to measure yourself or a sweater that fits well, to determine which size to make.

YARN SELECTION

For an exact reproduction of the projects photographed, use the yarn listed in the "Materials" section of the pattern. We've chosen yarns that are readily available in the U.S. and Canada at the time of printing. The Resources list on pages 86 and 87 provides addresses of yarn distributors. Contact them for the name of a retailer in your area.

YARN SUBSTITUTION

You may wish to substitute yarns. Perhaps you view small-scale projects as a chance to incorporate leftovers from your yarn stash, or the yarn specified may not be available in your area. You'll need to knit to the given gauge to obtain the knitted measurements with a substitute yarn (see

GAUGE

It is always important to knit a gauge swatch, and it is even more so with garments to ensure proper fit.

Patterns usually state gauge over a 4"/10cm span, however it's beneficial to make a larger test swatch. This gives a more precise stitch gauge, a better idea of the appearance and drape of the knitted fabric, and gives you a chance to familiarize yourself with the stitch pattern.

The type of needles used—straight- or double-pointed, wood or metal—will influence gauge, so knit your swatch with the needles you plan to use for the project. Measure gauge as illustrated. Try different needle sizes until your sample measures the required number of stitches and rows. *To get fewer stitches to the inch/cm, use larger needles; to get more stitches to the inch/cm, use smaller needles.*

Knitting in the round may tighten the gauge, so if you measured the gauge on a flat swatch, take another gauge reading after you begin knitting. When the piece measures at least 2"/5cm, lay it flat and measure over the stitches in the center of the piece, as the side stitches may be distorted.

It's a good idea to keep your gauge swatch in order to test blocking and cleaning methods.

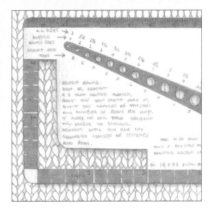

"Gauge" on this page). Be sure to consider how the fiber content of the substitute yarn will affect the comfort and the ease of care of your projects.

To facilitate yarn substitution, *Vogue Knitting* grades yarn by the standard stitch gauge obtained in stockinette stitch. You'll find a grading number in the "Materials" section of the pattern, immediately following the fiber type of the yarn. Look for a substitute yarn that falls into the same category. The suggested needle size and gauge on the ball band should be comparable to that on the Yarn Symbols chart (see page 16).

After you've successfully gauge-swatched a substitute yarn, you'll need to figure out how much of the substitute yarn the project requires. First, find the total length of the original yarn in the pattern (multiply number of balls by yards/meters per ball). Divide this figure by the new yards/meters per ball (listed on the ball band). Round up to the next whole number. The answer is the number of balls required.

FOLLOWING CHARTS

Charts are a convenient way to follow colorwork, lace, cable, and other stitch patterns at a glance. *Vogue Knitting* stitch charts utilize the universal knitting language of "symbolcraft." When knitting back and forth in rows, read charts from right to left on right side (RS) rows and from left to right on wrong side (WS) rows, repeating any stitch and row repeats as directed in the pattern. When knitting in the round, read charts from right to left on every round. Posting a self-adhesive note under your working row is an easy way to keep track of your place on a chart.

LACE

Lace knitting provides a feminine touch. Knitted lace is formed with "yarn overs," which create an eyelet hole in combination with decreases that create directional effects to make a yarn over (yo), merely pass the yarn over the right-hand needle to form a new loop. Decreases are worked as k2tog, ssk, or SKP depending on the desired slant and are spelled out specifically with each instruction. On the row or round that follows the lace or eyelet detail, each yarn over is treated as one stitch. If you're new to lace knitting, it's a good idea to count the stitches at the end of each row or round. Making a gauge swatch in the stitch pattern enables you to practice the lace pattern. Instead of binding off the swatch, place the final row on a holder, as the bind off tends to pull in the stitches and distort the gauge.

COLORWORK KNITTING

Two main types of colorwork are explored in this book.

INTARSIA

Intarsia is accomplished with separate bobbins of individual colors. This method is ideal for large blocks of color or for motifs that aren't repeated close together, such as the Flower Power Pullover (page 60). When changing colors, always pick up the new color and wrap it around the old color to prevent holes.

STRANDING

When motifs are closely placed, colorwork is accomplished by stranding along two or more colors per row, creating "floats" on the wrong side of the fabric. This technique is sometimes called Fair Isle knitting after the traditional Fair Isle patterns that are composed of small motifs with frequent color changes.

To keep an even tension and prevent holes while knitting, pick up yarns alternately over and under one another across or around. While knitting, stretch the stitches on the needle slightly wider than the length of the float at the back to keep work from puckering.

When changing colors at the beginning of rows or rounds, carry yarn along for a few rows only, or cut yarn and rejoin when needed. It is important to keep the "floats" small and neat so they don't catch when pulling on the piece.

BLOCKING

Blocking is an all-important finishing step in the knitting process. It is the best way to shape pattern pieces and smooth knitted edges in preparation for sewing together. Most garments retain their shape if the blocking stages in the instructions are followed carefully. Choose a blocking method according the the yarn care label and when in doubt, test-block your gauge swatch.

WET BLOCK METHOD

Using rust-proof pins, pin pieces to measurements on a flat surface and lightly dampen using a spray bottle. Allow to dry before removing pins.

STEAM BLOCK METHOD

With WS facing, pin pieces. Steam lightly, holding the iron 2"/5cm above the knitting. Do not press or it will flatten stitches.

FINISHING

The pieces in this book use a variety of finishing techniques from crocheting around the edges to embroidery at the neck. Directions for making pompoms are on page 15. Also refer to the illustrations provided for other useful techniques: the "wrap & turn" method of short row shaping, joining in the round, and three-needle bind-off.

CARE

Refer to the yarn label for the recommended cleaning method. Many of the projects in the book can be either washed by hand, or in the machine on a gentle or wool cycle, in lukewarm water with a mild detergent. Do not agitate, or soak for more than 10 minutes. Rinse gently with tepid water, then fold in a towel and gently press the water out. Lay flat to dry away from excess heat and light. Check the yarn band for any specific care instructions such as dry cleaning or tumble drying.

THREE-NEEDLE BIND-OFF

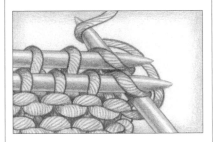

1 With RS placed together, hold pieces on two parallel needles. Insert a third needle knitwise into the first stitch of each needle, and wrap the yarn around the needle as if to knit.

2 Knit these two stitches together, and slip them off the needles. *Knit the next two stitches together in the same manner.

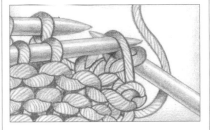

3 Slip the first stitch on the third needle over the second stitch and off the needle. Repeat from the * in Step 2 across the row until all stitches have been bound off.

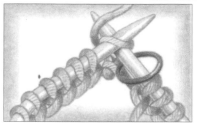

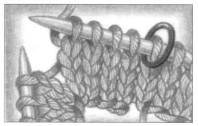

Hold the needle tip with the last cast-on stitch in your right hand and the tip with the first cast-on stitch in your left hand. Knit the first cast-on stitch, pulling the yarn tight to avoid a gap.

Work until you reach the marker. This completes the first round. Slip the marker to the right needle and work the next round.

SHORT ROW SHAPING
"WRAP AND TURN"

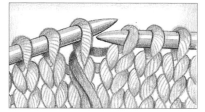

I To prevent holes in the piece and create a smooth transition, wrap a knit stitch as follows: With the yarn in back, slip the next stitch purlwise.

2 Move the yarn between the needle to the front of the work.

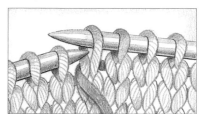

3 Slip the same stitch back to the left needle. Turn the work, bringing the yarn to the purl side between the needles. One stitch is wrapped.

4 When you have completed all the short rows, you must hide the wraps. Work to just before the wrapped stitch. Insert the right needles under the wrap and knitwise into the wrapped stitch. Knit them together.

POMPOM TEMPLATE

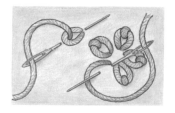

BULLION STITCH

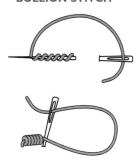

POMPOMS

1 Following the template, cut two circular pieces of cardboard.

2 Hold the two circles together and wrap the yarn tightly around the cardboard several times. Secure and carefully cut the yarn.

3 Tie a piece of yarn tightly between the two circles. Remove the cardboard and trim the pompom to the desired size.

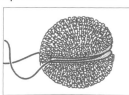

TWISTED CORD

1 If you have someone to help you, insert a pencil or knitting needle through each end of the strands. If not, place one end over a doorknob and put a pencil through the other end. Turn the strands clockwise until they are tightly twisted.

2 Keeping the strands taut, fold the piece in half. Remove the pencils and allow the cords to twist onto themselves.

KNITTING TERMS AND ABBREVIATIONS

approx approximately

beg begin(ning)

bind off Used to finish an edge and keep stitches from unraveling. Lift the first stitch over the second, the second over the third, etc. (UK: cast off)

cast on A foundation row of stitches placed on the needle in order to begin knitting.

CC contrast color

ch chain(s)

cm centimeter(s)

cont continu(e)(ing)

dc double crochet (UK: tr-treble)

dec decrease(ing)–Reduce the stitches in a row (knit 2 together).

dpn double-pointed needle(s)

foll follow(s)(ing)

g gram(s)

garter stitch Knit every row. Circular knitting: knit one round, then purl one round.

hdc half double crochet (UK: htr-half treble)

inc increase(ing)–Add stitches in a row (knit into the front and back of a stitch).

k knit

k2tog knit 2 stitches together

LH left-hand

lp(s) loop(s)

m meter(s)

MI make one stitch–With the needle tip, lift the strand between last stitch worked and next stitch on the left-hand needle and knit into the back of it. One stitch has been added.

YARN SYMBOLS

① **Fine Weight**
(29-32 stitches per 4"/10cm)
Includes baby and fingering yarns, and some of the heavier crochet cottons. The range of needle sizes is 0-4 (2-3.5mm).

② **Lightweight**
(25-28 stitches per 4"/10cm)
Includes sport yarn, sock yarn, UK 4-ply, and lightweight DK yarns. The range of needle sizes is 3-6 (3.25-4mm).

③ **Medium Weight**
(21-24 stitches per 4"/10cm)
Includes DK and worsted, the most commonly used knitting yarns. The range of needle sizes is 6-9 (4-5.5mm).

④ **Medium-heavy Weight**
(17-20 stitches per 4"/10cm)
Also called heavy worsted or Aran. The range of needle sizes is 8-10 (5-6mm).

⑤ **Bulky Weight**
(13-16 stitches per 4"/10cm)
Also called chunky. Includes heavier Icelandic yarns. The range of needle sizes is 10-11 (6-8mm).

⑥ **Extra-bulky Weight**
(9-12 stitches per 4"/10cm)
The heaviest yarns available. The range of needle sizes is 11 and up (8mm and up).

MC main color

mm millimeter(s)

no stitch On some charts, "no stitch" is indicated with shaded spaces where stitches have been decreased or not yet made. In such cases, work the stitches of the chart, skipping over the "no stitch" spaces.

oz ounce(s)

p purl

p2tog purl 2 stitches together

pat(s) pattern

pick up and knit (purl) Knit (or purl) into the loops along an edge.

pm place markers–Place or attach a loop of contrast yarn or purchased stitch marker as indicated.

psso pass slip stitch(es) over

rem remain(s)(ing)

rep repeat

rev St st reverse Stockinette stitch–Purl right-side rows, knit wrong-side rows. Circular knitting: purl all rounds. (UK: reverse stocking stitch)

rnd(s) round(s)

RH right-hand

RS right side(s)

sc single crochet (UK: dc-double crochet)

sk skip

SKP Slip 1, knit 1, pass slip stitch over knit 1.

SK2P Slip 1, knit 2 together, pass slip stitch over the knit 2 together.

sl slip–An unworked stitch made by passing a stitch from the left-hand to the right-hand needle as if to purl.

sl st slip stitch (UK: single crochet)

ssk slip, slip, knit–Slip next 2 stitches knitwise, one at a time, to right-hand needle. Insert tip of left-hand needle into fronts of these stitches from left to right. Knit them together. One stitch has been decreased.

sssk Slip next 3 sts knitwise, one at a time, to right-hand needle. Insert tip of left-hand needle into fronts of these stitches from left to right. Knit them together. Two stitches have been decreased.

st(s) stitch(es)

St st Stockinette stitch–Knit right-side rows, purl wrong-side rows. Circular knitting: knit all rounds. (UK: stocking stitch)

tbl through back of loop

tog together

WS wrong side(s)

wyib with yarn in back

wyif with yarn in front

work even Continue in pattern without increasing or decreasing. (UK: work straight)

yd yard(s)

yo yarn over–Make a new stitch by wrapping the yarn over the right-hand needle. (UK: yfwd, yon, yrn)

* = repeat directions following * as many times as indicated.

[ ] = Repeat directions inside brackets as many times as indicated.

DRAWSTRING TOP AND SKIRT

Cream of the cropped

Hip hugger! Circular-knit mini-skirt and cool cropped bell-sleeved top are both finished with cord drawstrings. Wrapped-stitch cabling gives a quilted look to this two-piece set designed by Teva Durham.

SIZES

Instructions are written for size 10. Changes for sizes 12 and 14 are in parentheses.

KNITTED MEASUREMENTS

Top
- Bust 29¼ (31½, 33¾)"/74.5 (80, 85.5)cm
- Length 14 (15, 15½)"/35.5 (38, 39.5)cm
- Upper arm 12 (13, 14¼)"/30.5 (33, 36)cm

Skirt
- Waist 23 (24½, 26)"/58.5 (62, 66)cm
- Length 16"/40.5cm

MATERIALS

Top
- 8 (8, 9) 1¾oz/50g balls (each approx 65yds/60m) of GGH/Muench Yarn *Goa* (cotton/acrylic④) in #13 blue

Skirt
- 5 (6, 7) balls in #13 blue
- One each size 8 (5mm) circular needle, 24"/60cm and 32"/80cm long *or size to obtain gauge*
- Cable needle
- Stitch holders and markers

GAUGES
- 14 sts and 20 rnds to 4"/10cm over rev St st using size 8 (5mm) needles.
- 21 sts to 4½"/11.5 cm over lattice pat using size 8 (5mm) needles.
Take time to check gauges.

Notes 1 Top and skirt are worked in the rnd. **2** Change to longer or shorter circular needle as needed.

LATTICE PAT
Worked in the rnd.
(multiple of 4 sts plus 1)
Rnds 1-7 [K1, p3] 5 times, k1.
Rnd 8 *Sl 5 sts to cn and hold to *front*, wrap yarn from back to front around sts on cn twice, (k1, p3, k1) from cn**, p3; rep from * once, rep between * and ** once.
Rnds 9-15 Rep rnds 1-7.
Rnd 16 K1, p3; rep from * of rnd 8 twice, k1.
Rep rnds 1-16 for lattice pat.

LATTICE PAT
Worked in rows (for sleeves).
(multiple of 4 sts plus 1)
Rows 1, 3, 5, 9, 11 and 13 (RS) [K1, p3] 5 times, k1.
Rows 2 and all WS rows [P1, k3] 5 times, p1.
Row 7 *Sl 5 sts to cn and hold to *front*, wrap yarn from back to front around sts on cn twice, (k1, p3, k1) from cn**, p3; rep from * once; rep between * and ** once.
Row 15 K1, p3; rep from * of row 7 twice, k1.

Row 16 Rep row 2.

Rep rows 1-16 for lattice pat.

TOP

BODY

Cast on 86 (94, 102) sts. Join, taking care not to twist sts on needle. Mark beg of rnd and sl marker every rnd. Work k1, p1 rib for 2"/5cm. Work 3 rnds in rev St st.

Next (inc) rnd Inc 1, p41 (45, 49), inc 1, pm (for side), inc 1, p41 (45, 49), inc 1. Rep last 4 rnds 3 times more—102 (110, 118) sts. Work even until piece measures 7"/18cm from beg. Place 51 (55, 59) sts on a holder for front and 51 (55, 59) sts on a holder for back.

SLEEVES

Cast on 53 (57, 61) sts. Work in k1, p1 rib for 3 rows.

Next row (RS) P16 (18, 20) work 21 sts in lattice pat, p16 (18, 20). Cont in pat as established, dec 1 st each side every 20th row 3 times—47 (51, 55) sts. Work even until piece measures 15½ (16, 16½)"/39.5 (40.5, 42)cm from beg. Place sts on a holder.

YOKE

Next (joining) rnd Work 46 (50, 54) sts from sleeve holder, pm, k2tog (last st of sleeve with first st from front), p49 (53, 57) sts from front holder, pm, k2tog (last st of front with first st from sleeve), work 45 (49, 53) sts of sleeve, pm, k2tog (last st of sleeve with first st from back), p49 (53, 57) sts, k2tog (last st of back with first st from sleeve)—192 (208, 224) sts.

Next (dec) rnd *P2tog, work to 2 sts before marker, p2tog, k1; rep from * around. Work 1 rnd even. Cont to work dec rnd every other rnd 10 (12, 14) times more—104 sts. Work in k1, p1 rib for 2"/5cm. Bind off loosely in rib.

FINISHING

Block pieces to measurements. Sew sleeve seams.

Make a twisted cord 38"/95cm long and thread through neckband.

SKIRT

Cast on 124 (130, 134) sts. Join, taking care not to twist sts on needle. Mark beg of rnd and sl marker every rnd. Work in k1, p1 rib for 3 rnds.

Beg lattice pat

Next rnd (RS) K1 (for side seam), p8 (9, 10), work 21 sts in lattice pat, p8 (9, 10), work 21 sts in lattice pat, p8 (9, 10), k1 (for side seam), p to end. Work 7 rnds even in pat as established.

Next (dec) rnd K1 side seam, p2tog, work in pat to 2 sts before side seam, p2tog, k1 side seam, p2tog, p to last 2 sts, p2tog. Rep dec rnd every 8th rnd 7 times—92 (98, 102) sts. Work even until piece measures 14"/35.5cm from beg.

Waistband

Work in k1, p1 rib for 2"/5cm. Bind off loosely in rib.

FINISHING

Block piece to measuresments. Make a twisted cord 38"/95cm long. Thread through waistband ribbing.

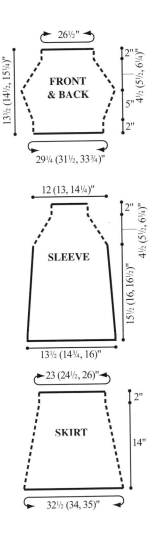

26½"

13½ (14½, 15¼)"

FRONT & BACK

2"

4½ (5½, 6¼)"

5"

2"

29¼ (31½, 33¾)"

12 (13, 14¼)"

2"

SLEEVE

4½ (5½, 6¼)"

15½ (16, 16½)"

13½ (14¾, 16)"

23 (24½, 26)"

2"

SKIRT

14"

32½ (34, 35)"

FINGERLESS GLOVES
High five

Hands off! Perfect for pounding the keyboard, these cool striped finger- and thumbless mitts, designed by Veronica Manno, knit up in a flash. Deep ribs make for a snug fit.

SIZES
One size.

MATERIALS
- 1 1¾oz/50g ball (each approx 105yd/96m) of Cleckheaton *Country 8-ply* by Plymouth Yarn (wool③) each in #1102 red (A), #2167 orange (B) and #1977 pink (C)
- One pair size 6 (4mm) needles *or size to obtain gauge*
- Stitch markers

GAUGE
20 sts and 28 rows to 4"/10cm over St st using size 6 (4mm) needles.
Take time to check gauge.

Stripe pattern
Work in St st as foll: *2 rows B, 2 rows C, 2 rows A; rep from * (6 rows) for stripe pat.

CUFF
With A, cast on 40 sts. Work in k2, p2 rib for 4"/10cm.

Hand
Work 4 rows in St st and stripe pat. Inc 1 st each side on next row, then every other row 4 times more—50 sts. Work even until piece measures 6"/15cm from beg. Change to A and work in k2, p2 rib for ¾"/2cm. Bind off in rib.

FINISHING
Block lightly. Sew side seam.

CROP TOP
Cut loose

Bare belly! The midriff style of this cropped top makes it perfect for any trend-conscious teen. Self-finished ribbed armholes, a stand-up neck, and a funky multi-colored yarn add style. Designed by Mari Lynn Patrick.

SIZES

Instructions are written for size 10. Changes for sizes 12 and 14 are in parentheses.

KNITTED MEASUREMENTS

■ Lower edge 23½ (25, 27)"/59.5 (63.5, 68.5)cm

■ Chest 29 (31, 32½)"/73.5 (78.5, 82.5)cm

■ Length 14 (15, 15½)"/35.5 (38, 39.5)cm

MATERIALS

■ 4 (4, 5) 1¾oz/50g balls (each approx 99yd/90m) of Trendsetter Yarns *Dolce* (acrylic myolis/polyamide ④) in #605 blue multi

■ One pair each sizes 9 and 10 (5.5 and 6mm) needles or size to obtain gauge

GAUGE

18 sts and 22 rows to 4"/10cm over St st using larger needles.
Take time to check gauge.

BACK

With smaller needles, cast on 53 (57, 61) sts. Work in k1, p1 rib for 3 rows. Change to larger needles. Beg with a p row, work in St st inc 1 st each side every 6th row 5 (4, 4) times, every 8th row 1 (2, 2) times— 65 (69, 73) sts. Work even until piece measures 8 (8½, 8½)"/20.5 (21.5, 21.5)cm from beg.

Armhole shaping

Bind off 4 sts at beg of next 2 rows.
Dec row (RS) P1, k1, p1, k1, p2tog, k to last 6 sts, p2tog, k1, p1, k1, p1.
Next row K1, p1, k1, p1, k1, p to last 5 sts, k1, p1, k1, p1, k1.
Next row Rep dec row. Then rep dec row every 2nd row once more, every 4th row 6 (7, 8) times, AT SAME TIME, when armhole measures 5 (5½, 6)"/12.5 (14, 15)cm, shape neck as foll.

Neck shaping

Next row (RS) Work to center 15 (15, 17) sts, join a 2nd ball of yarn and bind off center 15 (15, 17) sts, work to end. Working both sides at once, bind off 5 sts from each neck edge once. When armhole measures 6 (6½, 7)"/15 (16.5, 17.5)cm, bind off rem 7 (8, 8) sts each side for shoulders.

FRONT

Work as for back until armhole measures 3 (3½, 4)"/7.5 (9, 10)cm.

Neck shaping

Next row (RS) Work to center 11 (11, 13) sts, join a 2nd ball of yarn and bind off center 11 (11, 13) sts, work to end. Working both sides at once, bind off 2 sts from each neck edge twice, dec 1 st every other row 3 times. When same length as back, bind off 7 (8, 8) sts each side for shoulders.

FINISHING

Block pieces to measurements. Sew one shoulder seam.

Neckband

With smaller needles, pick up and k 73 (73, 77) sts evenly around neck edge.

Row 1 (WS) Beg with p1, work in k1, p1 rib, inc 16 sts evenly spaced around—89 (89, 93) sts. Cont in k1, p1 rib for 2¾"/7cm. Bind off in rib. Sew neckband and other shoulder seam. Sew side seams.

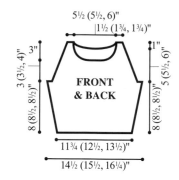

5½ (5½, 6)"

|1½ (1¾, 1¾)"

3"

1"

3 (3½, 4)"

8 (8½, 8½)"

5 (5½, 6)"

8 (8½, 8½)"

FRONT & BACK

11¾ (12½, 13½)"

14½ (15½, 16¼)"

Chunky monkey! Three weights of yarn create the bands as they move from bulky to ultra bulky in this wonderful weekend sweater. A big cowl neck makes it extra cozy for hanging out at the game. Designed by Veronica Manno.

SIZES

Instructions are written for size 10. Changes for sizes 12 and 14 are in parentheses.

KNITTED MEASUREMENTS

- Chest 39 (41, 43)"/99 (104, 109)cm
- Length 18½ (19½, 20½)"/47 (49.5, 52)cm
- Upper arm 15½ (16½, 17½)"/39.5 (42, 44.5)cm

MATERIALS

- 9 (9, 10) 1¾oz/100g balls (each approx 57yd/51m) of Classic Elite Yarns *Waterspun Weekend* (wool ⑥) in #7229 aqua (A)
- 4 (4, 5) 1¾oz/50g balls (each approx 138yd/123m) of *Waterspun* (wool ④) in #2546 aqua (B)
- One pair each sizes 11, 15 and 19 (8, 10 and 16mm) needles *or sizes to obtain gauges*

GAUGES

- 6 sts and 9 rows to 4"/10cm over St st using size 19 (16mm) needles and 2 strands of A held tog.
- 9 sts and 13 rows to 4"/10cm over St st using size 15 (10mm) needles and 1 strand of A.

- 12 sts and 16 rows to 4"/10cm over St st using size 11 (8mm) needles and 2 strands of B held tog.
Take time to check gauges.

BACK

With size 19 (16mm) needles and 2 strands of A held tog, cast on 29 (30, 32) sts. Work in St st for 4½"/11.5cm OR 10 rows. Cut 1 strand A. Change to size 15 (10mm) needles and work with 1 strand A only.

Next row (RS) With 1 strand A, knit, inc 15 (16, 16) sts evenly spaced across—44 (46, 48) sts. Work even until piece measures 10½ (11, 11½)"/26.5 (28, 29)cm from beg, end with a WS row. Cut A. Join 2 strands B and change to size 11 (8mm) needles.

Next row (RS) With 2 strands B, knit, inc 15 (16, 16) sts evenly spaced across—59 (62, 64) sts. P 1 row. Piece measures approx 11 (11½, 12)"/28 (29, 30.5)cm from beg.

Armhole shaping

Bind off 3 sts at beg of next 2 rows.
Next row (RS) K2, k2tog, k to last 4 sts, SKP, k2. P 1 row. Rep last 2 rows 3 (4, 4) times more—45 (46, 48) sts. Work even until armhole measures 7½ (8, 8½)"/19 (20.5, 21.5)cm. Bind off.

FRONT

Work as for back until armhole measures 5½ (6, 6½)"/14 (15, 16.5)cm.

Neck shaping

Next row (RS) K17 (17, 18), join a 2nd 2 strands of yarn and bind off center 11 (12,

12) sts, work to end. Working both sides at once, bind off 3 sts from each neck edge once, dec 1 st every other row 3 times—11 (11, 12) sts rem each side. Work even until same length as back to shoulders. Bind off sts each side for shoulders.

SLEEVES

With size 19 (16mm) needles and 2 strands of A held tog, cast on 14 sts. Work in St st for a total of 7½ (8½, 9½)"/19 (21.5, 24)cm, AT SAME TIME, inc 1 st each side every 6th row 2 (2, 3) times—18 (18, 20) sts. Cut 1 strand A. Change to size 15 (10mm) needles and cont with 1 strand A only.

Next row (RS) With 1 strand A, knit, inc 9 (9, 10) sts evenly spaced across—27 (27, 30) sts. Cont with 1 strand A until piece measures 13½ (14½, 15½)"/34 (37, 39.5)cm from beg, AT SAME TIME, inc 1 st each side every other row 0 (1, 1) time, every 4th row 4 times for 35 (37, 40) sts, end with a WS row. Cut A. Join 2 strands B and change to size 11 (8mm) needles.

Next row (RS) With 2 strands of B, knit, inc 11 (12, 12) sts evenly spaced—46 (49, 52) sts. Work even for 1 row.

Cap shaping

Bind off 3 sts at beg of next 2 rows.
Next row (RS) K2, k3tog, k to last 5 sts, SK2P, k2. P 1 row. Rep last 2 rows twice more.
Next row (RS) K2, k2tog, k to last 4 sts, SKP, k2. P 1 row. Rep last 2 rows 2 (3, 4) times more. Bind off 3 sts at beg of next 2

rows, 4 sts at beg of next 2 rows. Bind off rem 8 (9, 10) sts.

FINISHING

Block pieces to measurements. Sew one shoulder seam.

Turtleneck

With size 19 (16mm) needles and 2 strands of A held tog, pick up and k 55 (57, 57) sts evenly around neck edge. Work in k1, p1 rib for 6"/15cm. Bind off. Sew collar and shoulder seam. Sew sleeves into armholes. Sew side and sleeve seams.

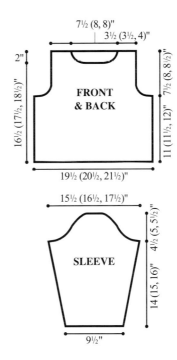

7½ (8, 8)"

3½ (3½, 4)"

2"

16½ (17½, 18½)"

FRONT & BACK

7½ (8, 8½)"

11 (11½, 12)"

19½ (20½, 21½)"

15½ (16½, 17½)"

4½ (5, 5½)"

SLEEVE

14 (15, 16)"

9½"

STRIPED STOCKING CAP
Freestylin'

Game boy! This lively striped stocking cap is worked in the round, making it a breeze to knit with no finishing required. Choose your favorite colors, your team stripes, or keep it solid. Designed by Jean Guirguis.

SIZE
One size.

MATERIALS
- 1 1¾oz/50g skein (each approx 110yds/100m) of Dale of Norway *Heilo* (wool③) each in #5545 purple (A), #9335 olive (B), #7562 green (C), #6135 turquoise (D), #7382 dk green (E) and #6545 teal (F)
- One each sizes 4 and 5 (3.5 and 3.75mm) circular needle, 16"/40cm long
- One set (5) size 5 (3.75mm) dpn
- Stitch markers

GAUGE
23 sts and 30 rnds to 4"/10cm over St st using larger needles.
Take time to check gauge.

STRIPE PATTERN
6 rows A, 6 rows B, 6 rows C, 6 rows D, 5 rows F, 5 rows B, 5 rows E, 5 rows A, 5 rows D, 5 rows C, 3 rows B, 3 rows F, 3 rows E, 3 rows D, 3 rows A, 3 rows C, 3 rows B, 3 rows E, 3 rows D, 3 rows F, 3 rows A, 3 rows C, 2 rows B, 2 rows D, 2 rows C, 2 rows A, 2 rows E, 2 rows F, 2 rows B, 2 rows A, 2 rows D, 2 rows C, 2 rows E, 2 rows F, 2 rows B, 2 rows A, 2 rows D, 2 rows C.

CAP
With smaller needle and A, cast on 104 sts. Join, taking care not to twist sts on needle. Mark end of rnd and sl marker every rnd. Work in rnds of k2, p2 rib for 3¼"/8cm. Cont in rnds of St st and stripe pat until piece measures 9¼"/23.5cm from beg, work last rnd as foll: k20, pm, k21, pm, k21, pm, k21, pm, k21, pm.

Next (dec) rnd *Work to marker, k2tog; rep from * around (5 sts dec'd). Work 3 rnds even. Rep last 4 rnds 17 times more—14 sts.

Next rnd K2tog around—7 sts. Pull yarn through rem sts and fasten tightly.

FINISHING
Block piece to measurements.
Make 3 pom poms in A, B and D and attach to top.

Nice 'n easy. Perfect for a beginning knitter, this ¾-sleeved garter-stitch cardigan works up in no time with just one simple stitch. Doubled yarn and minimal finishing make it even faster; a purchased applique is a cute addition to the pocket. Designed by Viola Carol.

SIZES

Instructions are written for size 10. Changes for sizes 12 and 14 are in parentheses.

KNITTED MEASUREMENTS

- Chest 34 (36, 38)"/86 (91.5, 96.5)cm
- Length 14½ (15½, 16)"/37 (39.5, 40.5)cm
- Upper arm 11 (11½, 12½)"/28 (29, 32)cm

MATERIALS

- 9 (10, 10) 1¾oz/50g balls (each approx 123yd/108m) of Reynolds/JCA *Saucy Sport* (cotton③) in #545 coral (A)
- 1 ball in #361 red (B)
- One pair size 11 (8mm) needles *or size to obtain gauge*
- Four 1⅛"/28mm buttons
- One 2½"/65mm purchased flower appliqué

GAUGE

14 sts and 26 rows to 4"/10cm over garter st using 2 strands of yarn and size 11 (8mm) needles.
Take time to check gauge.

Note

Work with 2 strands of yarn held tog throughout.

BACK

With 2 strands of A, cast on 60 (64, 68) sts. Work in k2, p2 rib for 1"/2.5cm, then cont in garter st until piece measures 8½ (9, 9)"/21.5 (23, 23)cm from beg.

Armhole shaping

Bind off 2 (3, 3) sts at beg of next 2 rows, dec 1 st each side every other row 2 (2, 3) times—52 (54, 56) sts. Work even until armhole measures 6 (6½, 7)"/15.5 (16.5, 17.5)cm. Bind off.

LEFT FRONT

With 2 strands of A, cast on 34 (36, 38) sts. Work in k2, p2 rib for 1"/2.5cm. Then, cont in garter st until piece measures 8½ (9, 9)"/21.5 (23, 23)cm from beg.

Armhole shaping

Next row (RS) Bind off 2 (3, 3) sts, k to end. Then dec 1 st at armhole edge every other row 2 (2, 3) times—30 (31, 32) sts. Work even until armhole measures 4¼ (4¾, 5¼)"/11 (12, 13.5)cm, end with a RS row.

Neck shaping

Next row (WS) Bind off 10 (11, 11) sts, k to end. Cont to bind off 2 sts from neck edge twice, dec 1 st every other row once. When same length as back, bind off rem 15 (15, 16) sts for shoulder. Place markers for 4 buttons on center edge, the first one just above rib, the last one at ¾"/2cm from neck edge, the others spaced evenly between.

RIGHT FRONT

Work as for left front reversing shaping and forming buttonholes opposite markers on RS rows by k2, yo, k2tog.

POCKET

With 2 strands B, cast on 5 sts.
Row 1 (RS) *K1 tbl; rep from * to end.
Row 2 Cast on 3 sts, p to end.
Row 3 Cast on 3 sts, k1 tbl in each st to end.
Row 4 Cast on 2 sts, p to end.
Row 5 Cast on 2 sts, k1 tbl in each st to end—15 sts. Work even as established until piece measures 4"/10cm from beg. Bind off.

SLEEVES

With 2 strands of A, cast on 30 (30, 34) sts. Work in k2, p2 rib for ½"/1cm. Then cont in garter st, inc 1 st each side every 10th row 4 (5, 5) times—38 (40, 44) sts. Work even until piece measures 9 (10½, 11½)"/23 (26.5, 29)cm for a ¾-length sleeve OR desired length to underarm.

Cap shaping

Bind off 2 sts at beg of next 8 rows, dec 1 st each side every other row 5 (6, 8) times. Bind off rem 12 sts.

FINISHING

Block pieces to measurements. Sew shoulder seams. Sew in sleeves. Sew side and sleeve seams. Sew appliqué on pocket. Sew pocket to lower right front. Sew on buttons.

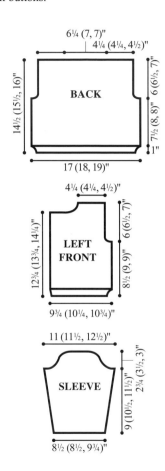

6¼ (7, 7)"
4¼ (4¼, 4½)"
BACK
14½ (15½, 16)"
6 (6½, 7)"
7½ (8, 8)"
1"
17 (18, 19)"

4¼ (4¼, 4½)"
LEFT FRONT
12¾ (13¾, 14¼)"
6 (6½, 7)"
8½ (9, 9)"
9¾ (10¼, 10¾)"

11 (11½, 12½)"
SLEEVE
9 (10½, 11½)"
2¾ (3½, 3)"
8½ (8½, 9¾)"

HOUNDSTOOTH VEST
Check it out

For Intermediate Knitters

Borrowed from the boys! Classic houndstooth-check patterning in a richly textured bouclé yarn adds style to this basic V-neck vest. Designed by **Rebbecca Rosen.**

SIZES

Instructions are written for size 10. Changes for sizes 12 and 14 are in parentheses.

KNITTED MEASUREMENTS

- Chest 30 (32, 33½)"/76 (81, 82.5)cm
- Length 18 (19½, 20½)"/45.5 (49.5, 52)cm

MATERIALS

- 4 (5, 6) 1¾oz/50g balls (each approx 84yds/77m) of Naturally/S.R. Kertzer *Café* (wool/alpaca/mohair/nylon③) in #712 ecru (A)
- 3 (4, 5) balls in #714 brown (B)
- One pair each sizes 8 and 9 (5 and 5.5mm) needles *or size to obtain gauge*
- Size 8 (5mm) circular needle, 16"/40cm long

GAUGE

18 sts and 19 rows to 4"/10cm over houndstooth pat using larger needles. *Take time to check gauge.*

HOUNDSTOOTH PATTERN

(multiple of 4 sts)
Row 1 (RS) K1 B, *k1 A, k3 B; rep from

* to last 3 sts, k1 A, k2 B.
Row 2 *P3 A, p1 B; rep from * to end.
Row 3 *K3 A, k1 B; rep from * to end.
Row 4 P1 B, *p1 A, p3 B; rep from * to last 3 sts, p1 A, p2 B.
Rep rows 1-4 for houndstooth pat.

BACK

With smaller needles and A, cast on 69 (75, 75) sts. Work in k3, p3 rib for 1½"/3.75cm, dec 1 (dec 3, inc 1) st on last WS row—68 (72, 76) sts. Change to larger needles and work in houndstooth pat until piece measures 10 (11, 11½)"/25.5 (28, 29)cm from beg.

Armhole shaping

Bind off 4 (5, 6) sts at beg of next 2 rows, 3 sts at beg of next 2 rows, 2 sts at beg of next 2 rows, dec 1 st each side every other row once—48 (50, 52) sts. Work even until armhole measures 7 (7½, 8)"/18 (19, 20.5)cm.

Neck and shoulder shaping

Bind off 5 sts at beg of next 4 rows, AT SAME TIME, bind off center 24 (26, 28) sts for neck, then bind off 2 sts from each neck edge once.

FRONT

Work as for back until armhole measures 2½"/6.5cm, end with a WS row.

Neck shaping

Next row (RS) Work 23 (24, 25) sts, join 2nd ball of yarn, k2tog and sl to a holder, work to end. Working both sides at once, dec 1 st at each neck edge *every* row 4 (5, 6) times, every other row 9 times—10 sts. Work even until piece measures same length as back to shoulders. Shape shoulders as for back.

FINISHING

Block pieces to measurement. Sew shoulder seams. Sew side seams.

Neckband

With RS facing, circular needle and A, pick up and k 24 (25, 26) sts along left front, pm, k1 from holder, pm, 24 (25, 26) along right front and 23 (27, 31) sts along back neck—72 (78, 84) sts. Join and work in rnds of k3, p3 rib as foll: rib to 2 sts before marker, SKP, k center st, k2tog, rib to end. Rep this rnd 3 times more. Bind off loosely in rib.

Armhole band

With RS facing, circular needle and A, pick up and k 66 (72, 78) sts evenly around armhole. Join and work in rnds of k3, p3 rib for 4 rnds. Bind off loosely in rib.

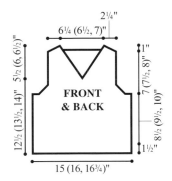

2¼"

6¼ (6½, 7)"

5½ (6, 6½)"

12½ (13½, 14)"

FRONT & BACK

1"

7 (7½, 8)"

8½ (9½, 10)"

1½"

15 (16, 16¾)"

EMBROIDERED CARDIGAN
Covent Garden

London calling! This classic school-girl cardigan, complete with full-fashioning and bouillon stitch embroidery, is quick-to-knit in a soft, bulky-weight yarn. Designed by Mari Lynn Patrick.

SIZES

Instructions are written for size 10. Changes for sizes 12 and 14 are in parentheses.

KNITTED MEASUREMENTS

- Chest 33 (35, 38)"/84 (89, 96.5)cm
- Length 18½ (19½, 21)"/47 (49.5, 53)cm
- Upper arm 11½ (12, 13¼)"/29 (30.5, 33.5)cm

MATERIALS

- 10 (11, 12) 1¾oz/50g balls (each approx 74yd/m) of Reynolds/JCA *Contessa* (lambswool/angora/nylon⑤) in #21 lilac (MC)
- 2 balls in #84 beige (CC)
- One pair each sizes 9 and 10½ (5.5 and 7mm) needles or size to obtain gauge
- Six ¾"/20mm buttons
- Embroidery floss in lt pink, dk pink, burgundy, bright green, pale yellow, lt rust and dark rust
- Embroidery needle

GAUGE

13 sts and 18 rows to 4"/10cm over St st using larger needles.
Take time to check gauge.

BACK

With smaller needles and CC, cast on 53 (58, 63) sts.
Row 1 (RS) K3, *p2, k3; rep from * to end. Cont in k3, p2 rib for 6 rows more. Change to larger needles and with MC, p 1 row on WS, inc 1 (0, dec 1) st—54 (58, 62) sts. Work even in St st until piece measures 11½ (12, 13)"/29 (30.5, 33)cm from beg.

Armhole shaping

Bind off 2 (3, 4) sts at beg of next 2 rows.
Dec row (RS) K3, k3tog, k to last 6 sts, SK2P, k3. Rep dec row every 4th row twice more—38 (40, 42) sts. Work even until armhole measures 6 (6½, 7)"/15 (16.5, 18)cm from beg.

Neck and shoulder shaping

Bind off 3 (4, 4) sts at beg of next 4 rows, 4 (3, 3) sts at beg of next 2 rows. Bind off rem 18 (18, 20) sts.

LEFT FRONT

With smaller needles and CC, cast on 30 (30, 32) sts.
Row 1 (RS) K1 (2, 2), *p2, k3; rep from *, end p2, k0 (1, 3). Cont in k3, p2 rib for 6 rows more. Change to larger needles and with MC, p 1 row on WS, dec 2 (0, 0) sts—28 (30, 32) sts. Work even in St st until piece measures 11½ (12, 13)"/29 (30.5, 33)cm from beg.

Armhole shaping

Next row (RS) Bind off 2 (3, 4) sts, work to end. P 1 row.

Dec row (RS) K3, k3tog, k to end. Rep dec row every 4th row twice more—20 (21, 22) sts. Work even until armhole measures 4¼ (4¾, 5¼)"/11 (12, 13.5)cm, end with a RS row.

Neck shaping
Next row (WS) Bind off 3 (3, 4) sts, work to end. Cont to shape neck binding off 3 sts from neck edge twice, dec 1 st once. Work even until same length as back to shoulder. Bind off 3 (4, 4) sts from armhole edge twice, 4 (3, 3) sts once.

RIGHT FRONT
Work as for left front reversing shaping.

SLEEVES
With smaller needles and CC, cast on 27 sts. **Row 1 (RS)** K1, *k3, p2; rep from *, end k1. Cont in k3, p2 rib for 6 rows more. Change to larger needles and with MC, p 1 row on WS. Cont in St st, inc 1 st each side every 8th row 5 (6, 8) times—37 (39, 43) sts. Work even until piece measures 14½ (15½, 16½)"/37 (39.5, 42)cm from beg.

Cap shaping
Bind off 3 (3, 4) sts at beg of next 2 rows, 2 sts a beg of next 2 rows. Dec 1 st each side every other row 5 (6, 7) times. Bind off 2 sts at beg of next 4 rows. Bind off rem 9 sts.

FINISHING
Block pieces to measurements. Sew shoulder seams.

Left front band
With smaller needles and CC, pick up and k 68 (73, 78) sts evenly along left front edge.
Row 1 (WS) P3, *k2, p3; rep from * to end. Work in k2, p3 rib for 3 rows more. Bind off in rib. Place markers for 5 buttons, the first one at ¾"/2cm from lower edge, the top one at 1½"/4cm from neck edge and the others evenly spaced between.

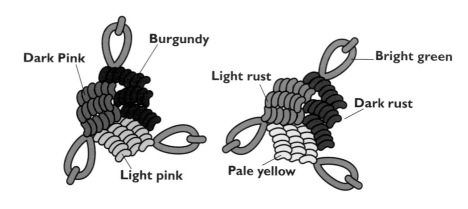

Dark Pink · Burgundy · Light rust · Bright green · Dark rust · Light pink · Pale yellow

Right front band

Work as for left front band working buttonholes opposite markers on row 3 by yo, p2tog (or k2tog) opposite markers.

Neckband

With smaller needles and CC, pick up and k 64 (64, 69) sts evenly around neck edge.
Row 1 (WS) K3, *p3, k2; rep from *, end k1. Work 1 row even.
Next row Work 1 more buttonhole in right front neck by k2tog, yo. Work 1 row even. Bind off. Sew sleeves into armholes. Sew side and sleeve seams.

Embroidery

Foll diagram, embroider flowers around front neck in colors foll photo. Flowers are worked in bouillon st and leaves in lazy daisy st.

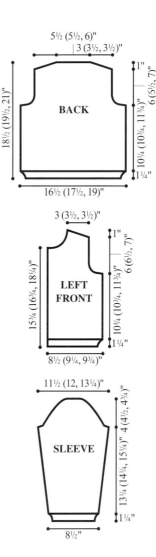

5½ (5½, 6)"

3 (3½, 3½)"

1"

6 (5½, 7)"

18½ (19½, 21)"

BACK

10¼ (10¾, 11¾)"

1¼"

16½ (17½, 19)"

3 (3½, 3½)"

1"

6 (6½, 7)"

15¾ (16¾, 18¼)"

LEFT FRONT

10¼ (10¾, 11¾)"

1¼"

8½ (9¼, 9¾)"

11½ (12, 13¼)"

4 (4½, 4¾)"

SLEEVE

13¼ (14¼, 15¼)"

1¼"

8½"

SLEEVELESS MOHAIR PULLOVER
Girls in the hood

Very Easy Very Vogue

Soft focus. Fuzzy mohair in fun shades of pink and a cool cross-over hood give cozy warmth to this sleeveless top. It's so easy, teens can try this one themselves. Designed by Kristin Spurkland.

SIZES
Instructions are written for size 10. Changes for sizes 12 and 14 are in parentheses.

KNITTED MEASUREMENTS
- Chest 32½ (35, 36½)"/82.5 (89, 92.5)cm
- Length 17¾ (19, 20½)"/45 (48.5, 52)cm

MATERIALS
- 3 (3, 4) 1¾oz/50g balls (each approx 105yd/95m) of Garnstudio/Aurora Yarns *Vienna* (mohair/polyester ⑤) in #28 dk pink (A)
- 2 (2, 3) balls in #36 lt pink (B)
- One pair size 10 (6mm) needles *or size to obtain gauge*
- Size 10 (6mm) circular needle, 24"/60cm long
- Stitch holders

GAUGE
15 sts and 20 rows to 4"/10cm over St st using size 10 (6mm) needles.
Take time to check gauge.

BACK
With A, cast on 59 (65, 68) sts.
Row 1 (WS) P2, *k1, p2; rep from * to end.
Row 2 K2, *p1, k2; rep from * to end.
Rep row 1 once, inc 2 (0, 0) sts on this row—61 (65, 68) sts. Work in St st until piece measures 11 (12, 13¼)"/28 (30.5, 33.5)cm from beg.

Armhole shaping
Bind off 4 sts at beg of next 2 rows.
Dec row (RS) K2, ssk, k to last 4 sts, k2tog, k2. Change to B and p 1 row. Then, cont with B, working dec row on next row then every other row 1 (2, 3) times more—47 (49, 50) sts. Work even until armhole measures 6¾ (7, 7¼)"/17 (18, 18.5)cm.

Neck and shoulders
Next row (RS) Bind off 11 (12, 12) sts, k center 25 (25, 26) sts and sl to a holder for neck, bind off rem 11 (12, 12) sts.

FRONT
Work as for back through last row in A. With B, p 1 row, then work dec row with B—49 (53, 56) sts.

Divide for neck
Next row (WS) P31 (33, 34), sl rem 18 (20, 22) sts to a holder to be worked later. Cont on right side only, dec 1 st at armhole edge every other row 1 (2, 3) times more—30 (31, 31) sts. Work even until armhole measures 6¾ (7, 7¼)"/17 (18,

18.5)cm. Bind off 11 (12, 12) sts from armhole edge and sl rem 19 sts to a holder for hood.

Left side

Working from WS from behind the sts of right side, pick up and p 13 (13, 12) sts behind these sts, then p across 18 (20, 22) sts from holder—31 (33, 34) sts. Work armhole decs and cont as on right side to shoulder. Bind off 11 (12, 12) sts from armhole edge and sl rem 19 sts to a holder for hood.

Block pieces to measurements. Sew shoulder seams. Sew side seams.

Hood

With circular needle and B, work across 19 sts of right side of front neck, pick up and k 1 st at shoulder, 25 (25, 26) sts from back neck holder, 2 (2, 1) sts at shoulder, 19 sts from left side of front neck—66 sts. Work in St st for 10 (11, 12)"/25.5 (28, 30.5)cm, end with a RS row. Place 33 sts on 2 needles and work 3-needle bind-off working seam tog.

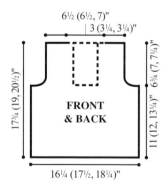

6½ (6½, 7)"

3 (3¼, 3¼)"

17¾ (19, 20½)"

11 (12, 13¼)"   6¾ (7, 7¼)"

FRONT & BACK

16¼ (17½, 18¼)"

CROPPED CABLE PULLOVER

Aran attitude

Cable queen. Spiralling diagonal twists form the background of this charming cropped Aran-style pullover. A classic horseshoe cable adorns the front and sleeves. Designed by Shirley Paden.

SIZES

Instructions are written for size 10. Changes for sizes 12 and 14 are in parentheses.

KNITTED MEASUREMENTS

■ Bust 30 (34, 36)"/76 (86.5, 91.5)cm
■ Length 15½ (16½, 17½)"/39 (42, 44.5)cm
■ Upper arm 11 (12½, 14)"/28 (32, 35.5)cm

MATERIALS

■ 10 (12, 14) 1¾oz/50g skeins (each approx 85yds/78m) of Berroco, Inc. *Cotton Twist* (cotton/rayon④) in #8335 blue
■ One pair each sizes 6 and 7 (4 and 4.5mm) needles *or size to obtain gauge*
■ Size 6 (4mm) circular needle, 16"/40cm long
■ Cable needle

GAUGES

■ 24 sts and 29 rows to 4"/10cm over twist st pat using size 7 (4.5mm) needles.
■ 18 sts to 2"/5cm over ribbed cable pat using size 7 (4.5mm) needles.
Take time to check gauges.

Note Work k1 selvage sts at each end of every row. Selvage sts are not figured into the finished measurements.

STITCH GLOSSARY

Right Twist (RT)
K2tog and leave sts on RH needle; then insert RH needle from front between the 2 sts just k tog and k the first st again; then sl both sts from needle tog.

Twist Stitch Pattern
(multiple of 3 sts)
Row 1 (RS) *RT, k1; rep from * to end.
Rows 2 and 4 Purl.
Row 3 *K1, RT; rep from * to end.
Rep rows 1-4 for twist st pat.

Ribbed Cable Pattern
(Panel of 18 sts)
Rows 1, 3, 5 and 9 (RS) P1, k1, [p2, k2] 3 times, p2, k1, p1.
Row 2 and all WS rows K1, p1, [k2, p2] 3 times, k2, p1, k1.
Row 7 P1, sl 4 sts to cn and hold to *back*, k1, p2, k1, (k1, p2, k1) from cn, sl 4 sts to cn and hold to *front*, k1 p2, k1, (k1, p2, k1) from cn, p1.
Row 10 Rep row 2.
Rep rows 1-10 for ribbed cable pat.

BACK

With smaller needles, cast on 98 (110, 116) sts. Work in k1, p1 rib for 2"/5cm, end with a RS row. P 1 row. Change to larger needles.

Next row (RS) K1 (selvage st), work 39 (45, 48) sts in twist st pat, 18 sts in ribbed cable pat, 39 (45, 48) sts in twist st pat, k1 (selvage st). Work even in pats as established until piece measures 9 (9½, 10)"/23 (24, 25.5)cm from beg, end with a WS row.

Armhole shaping
Bind off 2 (3, 3) sts at beg of next 2 rows, 1 (2, 2) sts at beg of next 8 (2, 2) rows, 0 (1, 1) st at beg of next 0 (8, 8) rows—86 (92, 98) sts. Work even until armhole measures 6½ (7, 7½)"/16.5 (18, 19)cm from beg. Bind off.

Work as for back until piece measures 13 (14, 15)"/33 (35.5, 38)cm from beg.

Neck shaping
Next row (RS) Work 34 (37, 40) sts, join a 2nd ball of yarn and bind off center 18 sts, work to end. Working both sides at once, cont to bind off at each neck edge 4 sts once, 3 sts once, 2 sts twice, then dec 1 st each side every other row twice—21 (24, 27) sts each side. Work even until same length as back to shoulder. Bind off.

With smaller needles, cast on 50 (56, 56) sts. Work in k1, p1 rib for 2"/5cm, end with a RS row. P 1 row. Change to larger needles.
Next row (RS) K1 (selvage st), work 15 (18, 18) sts in twist st pat, 18 sts in ribbed cable pat, 15 (18, 18) sts in twist st pat, k1 (selvage st). Cont in pats as established, inc 1 st each side every 4th row 6 (7, 15) times,

every 6th row 6 (7, 3) times—74 (84, 92) sts. Work even until piece measures 12 (13½, 14½)"/ 30.5 (34, 37)cm from beg.

Cap shaping
Bind off 0 (3, 3) sts at beg of next 2 rows, 2 sts at beg of next 16 (2, 2) rows, 0 (3, 3) sts at beg of next 2 rows, 0 (2, 2) sts at beg of next 0 (12, 16) rows, then dec 1 st each side every other row 4 times, bind off 4 sts at beg of next 4 rows. Bind off rem 18 (20, 20)sts.

Block pieces to measurements. Sew shoulder seams.

Neckband
With RS facing and circular needle, pick up and k 98 sts evenly around neck edge. Work in k1, p1 rib for 1½"/4cm. Bind off loosely in rib.

Set in sleeves. Sew side and sleeve seams.

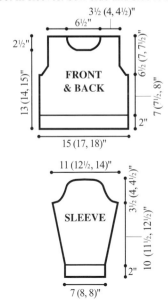

BOY'S WEEKEND PULLOVER

Hangin' out

No sweat! Great for both girls and guys, this raglan-sleeved pullover sports garter stitch edges, a cool kangaroo pocket and shaped shawl collar. Design from the Cleckheaton Design Studio.

SIZES

Instructions are written for size 10. Changes for sizes 12 and 14 are in parentheses.

KNITTED MEASUREMENTS

■ Chest 36 (38½, 41)"/91.5 (98, 104)cm
■ Length 20 (22, 23)"/51 (56, 58.5)cm
■ Upper arm 14 (15, 15½)"/35.5 (38, 39.5)cm

MATERIALS

■ 12 (13, 14) 1¾oz/50g balls (each approx 105yds/96m) Cleckheaton *Country Naturals 8-ply* by Plymouth Yarn (wool③) in #1456 green
■ One pair size 6 (4mm) needles *or size to obtain gauge*
■ One extra size 6 (4mm) needle
■ Stitch holders

GAUGE

22 sts and 30 rows to 4"/10cm over St st using size 6 (4mm) needles.
Take time to check gauge.

Note Collar is shaped using short rows. To avoid holes, use the wrap & turn method describe in the Basics section.

BACK

Cast on 97 (103, 109) sts. Beg with a WS row, work 10 rows in garter st, inc 3 sts evenly across last RS row—100 (106, 112) sts. Work in St st until piece measures 12 (13½, 14)"/30.5 (34.5, 35.5)cm from beg.

Armhole shaping

Bind off 2 sts at beg of next 2 rows, [dec 1 st each side *every* row 3 times, work 1 row even] 7 times—54 (60, 66) sts. Dec 1 st each side every other row 15 (17, 19) times—24 (26, 28) sts. P 1 row. Bind off.

POCKET LINING

Cast on 60 sts. Work in St st for 10 rows. Sl sts to a holder.

FRONT

Cast on 97 (103, 109) sts. Beg with a WS row, work in garter st for 10 rows, inc 3 sts evenly across last RS row—100 (106, 112) sts. Then work in St st for 9 rows.

Pocket

Next row (RS) K80 (83, 86), sl rem 20 (23, 26) sts to a holder, turn and p60, sl rem 20 (23, 26) sts to a holder. Cont on these 60 sts only (for pocket), dec 1 st each side every 4th row 9 times—42 sts. P 1 row, place sts on a holder.
Next row (RS) Work across 20 (23, 26) sts from holder, 60 sts from pocket lining holder, 20 (23, 26) sts from holder—100 (106, 112) sts. Beg with a WS row, work in St st for 35 rows.

Join pocket

Next row (RS) K29 (32, 35), with 42 pocket sts held to RS of front, join by k2tog (1 st from pocket with one st from front) across all pocket sts, knit to end. Cont as for back until piece measures same as back to armhole.

Neck and armhole shaping

Shape armhole as for back, AT SAME TIME, when armhole measures 2½"/6.5cm, shape neck as foll: join a 2nd ball of yarn and bind off center 8 sts. Working both sides at once, dec 1 st at each neck edge every 4th 4 (4, 6) times, every 6th row 4 (5, 4) times—2 sts each side. K2tog, fasten off.

SLEEVES

Cast on 44 (46, 48) sts. Beg with a WS row, work in garter st for 9 rows. Then cont in St st, inc 1 st each side every 4th row 3 (4, 4) times, every 6th row 13 (14, 15) times—76 (82, 86) sts. Work even until piece measures 13½ (15, 16)"/34 (38, 40.5)cm from beg.

Cap shaping

Bind off 2 sts at beg of next 2 rows, [dec 1 st each side *every* row 3 times, work 1 row even] 4 (5, 4) times, then dec 1 st each side every other row 21 (21, 25,) times—6 (6, 8) sts. P 1 row. Bind off.

COLLAR

Cast on 5 sts. K 1 row on WS. Work in garter st, inc 1 st at beg of next row, then every 4th row 17 (15, 9) times, every 6th row 1 (3, 9) times—24 sts. Work 2 rows even.

Beg short row shaping

*K18, w & t, k to end. Work 4 rows even across all sts. Rep from * 10 (11, 12) times, then turn and work 1 row even. Cont in garter st, dec 1 st at beg of next row, then every 6th row 0 (2, 8) times, every 4th row 18 (16, 10) times—5 sts. Bind off.

FINISHING

Block pieces to measurements.

Pocket edges

With RS facing, pick up and knit 26 sts evenly along shaped edge of pocket. Work 5 rows in garter st. Bind off loosely. Rep for other side of pocket. Sew pocket edges to front.

Sew raglan sleeve caps to raglan armholes. Sew side and sleeve seams. Sew shaped edge of collar to neck, sewing ends to bound-off sts at center front.

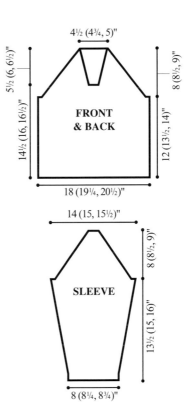

4½ (4¾, 5)"

5½ (6, 6½)"

8 (8½, 9)"

14½ (16, 16½)"

FRONT & BACK

12 (13½, 14)"

18 (19¼, 20½)"

14 (15, 15½)"

8 (8½, 9)"

SLEEVE

13½ (15, 16)"

8 (8¼, 8¾)"

SPIRAL CAP
Swirl pool

Twist and shout! A simple slanted pattern stitch creates the fetching swirl, as well as the shaping, on this clever cap. Worked in the round, it features a knotted I-cord at the top. Designed by Lipp Holmfeld.

SIZE
One size.

MATERIALS
- 1 3½oz/100g skein (each approx 66yds/60m) of Lane Borgosesia *Delphi* (wool/acrylic⑥) in #202 red
- One each sizes 10½ and 11 (7 and 8mm) circular needle, 16"/40cm long *or size to obtain gauge*
- One set (5) size 11 (8mm) dpn
- Stitch markers

GAUGE
12 sts and 13 rnds to 4"/10cm over St st, using larger needles.
Take time to check gauge.

Notes
1 Piece is shown in reverse St st. For ease in working, work in St st and turn inside out at completion.
2 Change to dpn when there are too few sts to fit comfortably on the circular needle.

K1, P1 Twisted Rib
Rnd 1 *K1 tbl, p1; rep from * around.
Rep rnd 1 for k1, p1 twisted rib.

CAP
With smaller needle, cast on 56 sts. Join, taking care not to twist sts on needle. Mark end of rnd and sl marker every rnd. Work in k1, p1 rib twisted rib for 4 rnds. Turn piece to WS. Change to larger needle and k 2 rnds.

Beg slant pat
Rnd 1 *SKP, k4, yo, k2; rep from * around.
Rep this rnd 15 times more.
Next (dec) rnd *SKP, k6; rep from * around.
Next (dec) rnd *SKP, k5; rep from * around.
Next (dec) rnd *SKP, k4; rep from * around.
Change to dpn and cont to dec in this way until 14 sts rem.
Next (dec) rnd SKP around—7 sts.
Place rem sts on 2 dpn and work I-cord as foll: *slide sts to beg of needle without turning, k7; rep from * 4 times more. Pull yarn through rem 7 sts. Draw up tightly and fasten off.

FINISHING
Block piece. Turn piece so that reverse St st side is showing. Pull top of I-cord into center to form button (see photo).

PINK PULLOVER

Star-studded

Super star! Emily Westman sketched her dream pullover for designer Mom, Betsy Westman, to knit for her. The studded star, pink mohair and bell-sleeves give it that cool 70's look!

SIZES

Instructions are written for size 8. Changes for sizes 10, 12 and 14 are in parentheses.

KNITTED MEASUREMENTS

- Chest 35 (37, 39½, 42)"/89 (94, 100.5, 106.5)cm
- Length 17 (18, 19½, 21)"/43 (46, 49.5, 53.5)cm
- Upper arm 16 (16½, 17, 18)"/40.5 (42, 43, 45.5)cm

MATERIALS

- 3 (4, 4, 5) skeins (each approx 222yds/203m) of Lion Brand Yarns Co. *Imagine* (acrylic/mohair④) in #101 pink
- One pair each sizes 9 and 10 (5.5 and 6mm) needles *or size to obtain gauge*
- Size 9 (5.5mm) circular needle, 16"/40cm long
- Stitch markers
- 20 nailhead studs for star

GAUGE

15 sts and 20 rows to 4"/10 cm over St st using larger needles.
Take time to check gauge.

BACK

With smaller needles, cast on 66 (70, 74, 78) sts. Work 2 rows garter st. Change to larger needles and work in St st, dec 1 st each side every 4th row 3 times—60 (64, 68, 72) sts. Work even until piece measures 3"/7.5cm from beg. Place marker at waist. Then inc 1 st each side every 8th (10th, 12th, 14th) row 3 times—66 (70, 74, 78) sts. Work even until piece measures 9 (10, 11, 12)"/23 (25.5, 28, 30.5)cm from beg.

Armhole shaping

Bind off 3 sts beg next 2 rows, dec 1 st each side *every* row twice, then every other row once—54 (58, 62, 66) sts. Work even until armhole measures 8 (8, 8½, 9)"/20.5 (20.5, 21.5, 23) cm. Bind off.

FRONT

Work as for back until armhole measures 5 (5, 5½, 6)"/12.5 (12.5, 14, 15)cm.

Neck shaping

Next row (RS) Work 22 (23, 25, 26) sts, join 2nd ball of yarn and bind off center 10 (12, 12, 14) sts, work to end. Working both sides at once, bind off 3 sts from each neck edge once, then dec 1 st *every* row twice, then every other row 3 times—14 (15, 17, 18) sts. Work even until piece measures same as back. Bind off.

SLEEVES

With smaller needles, cast on 46 (48, 50,

52) sts. Work 2 rows garter st. Change to larger needles and work in St st, dec 1 st each side every 4th (4th, 6th, 6th) row 4 times—38 (40, 42, 44) sts. Work even until piece measures 4 (4, 5, 5)"/10 (10, 12.5, 12.5)cm from beg. Place markers at each side. Then inc 1 st each side every 4th row 8 (6, 5, 6) times and every 6th row 3 (5, 6, 6) times—60 (62, 64, 68) sts. Work even until piece measures 14 (15, 16½, 17)"/35.5 (38, 42, 43) cm from beg, end with a WS row.

Cap shaping
Bind off 4 sts at beg of next 2 rows, 2 sts at beg of next 2 rows, 1 st at beg of next 4 rows—44 (46, 48, 52) sts. Work 2 rows even. Bind off.

FINISHING
Block pieces to measurements.
Place studs on front foll chart. Sew shoulder seams. Set in sleeves. Sew sleeve and side seams making sure st markers correspond.

Neckband
With RS facing and circular needle, pick up and k 70 (74, 74, 78) sts evenly around neck. Work 3 rnds garter st as foll: P 1 rnd, k 1 rnd, p 1 rnd. Bind off loosely knitwise.

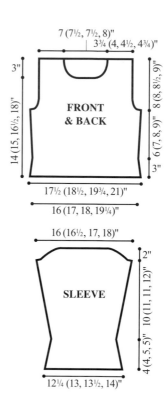

7 (7½, 7½, 8)"
3¾ (4, 4½, 4¾)"
3"
FRONT & BACK
14 (15, 16½, 18)"
8 (8, 8½, 9)"
6 (7, 8, 9)"
3"
17½ (18½, 19¾, 21)"
16 (17, 18, 19¼)"

16 (16½, 17, 18)"
2"
SLEEVE
10 (11, 11, 12)"
4 (4, 5, 5)"
12¼ (13, 13½, 14)"

TUBE TOP
Disco diva

For Intermediate Knitters

Dancing queen. This chic little tube is knit from the top down in a fun diagonal stripe pattern. Add an easy I-cord tie to make a halter. Designed by Gayle Bunn.

SIZES
Instructions are written for size 8/10. Changes for size 12/14 are in parentheses.

KNITTED MEASUREMENTS
- Chest 28 (32)"/70 (80)cm
- Length 16½ (18)"/41.25 (45)cm

MATERIALS
- 2 (3) 1¾oz/50g balls (each approx 136yd/125m) of Patons® *Grace* (cotton③) in #60322 lilac (A)
- 2 (2) balls in #60733 turquoise (B)
- One pair each sizes 3 and 5 (3 and 3.75mm) needles *or size to obtain gauge*
- Size G/6 (4mm) crochet hook
- Stitch marker

GAUGE
24 sts and 32 rows to 4"/10cm over St st using larger needles.
Take time to check gauge.

STRIPE PATTERN
Work in St st as foll: *2 rows A, 2 rows B; rep from * (4 rows) for stripe pat.

BACK

Section I
Beg at upper edge, with larger needles and A, cast on 3 sts. P 1 row.
Next row [Inc 1 in next st] twice, k1—5 sts. P 1 row.
Next (inc) row Inc 1 (in first st), k to last 2 sts, inc 1, k1—7 sts. P 1 row. Cont as established, rep last 2 rows 22 (24) times more—51 (55) sts, end with a WS row. Sl sts to a holder.

Section 2
Work as for section 1, do *not* break yarn.

Joining row
Next row (RS) Cont on Section 2 in pat as established, inc 1 (in first st), k48 (52), ssk, pm, work across sts from first holder as foll: k2tog, k to last 2 sts, inc 1, k1—102 (110) sts. P 1 row. Rep last 2 rows until piece measures 10½ (11)"/26.5 (28)cm, end with a WS row.

Edge shaping
Next row (RS) Ssk, work to 2 sts before marker, ssk, sl marker, k2tog, work to last 2 sts, k2tog. P 1 row. Rep last 2 rows until 4 sts rem. P4tog. Fasten off.

FRONT
Work as for back.

FINISHING
Block pieces to measurements.

Edging

With RS facing, smaller needles and A, pick up and k 80 (88) sts along lower edge of back. Work in k1, p1 rib for 1¼"/3cm. Bind off in rib. Work in same way on front.

Back casing

With RS facing, smaller needles and A, pick up and k 80 (88) sts along upper edge of back. Beg with a WS row, work 7 rows in St st. Bind off.

Front casing

With RS facing, smaller needles and A, pick up and k 80 (88) sts across front. P 1 row.

Drawstring opening

Next row (RS) K38 (40), k2tog, yo twice, ssk, k to end. **Next row** P, working into each double yo as foll: p into first lp, p into back of 2nd lp. Cont in St st for 4 rows more Bind off.

DRAWSTRING

With 2 strands of A and crochet hook, make a ch 38 (40)"/96.5 (101.5)cm long. Fasten off.

NECK TIE

With 2 strands of A and crochet hook, make a chain approx 32 (34)"/81 (86.5cm)cm long. Fasten off.

Sew side seams. Fold upper edging to WS and to form casing and sew in place. Thread drawstring through casing. Knot end and tie in a knot at center front. Fold neck tie in half and sew to inside of casing at center front.

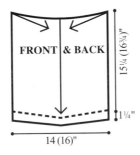

FRONT & BACK

15¼ (16¾)"

1¼"

14 (16)"

Bohemian Babe! Hip flowers bloom across the front and back of this retro tunic-length pullover. Designed by Bonnie Franz, it is quick to knit and extra cozy in chunky wool yarn.

SIZES
Instructions are written for size 10. Changes for sizes 12 and 14 are in parentheses.

KNITTED MEASUREMENTS
- Chest 43 (46, 49½)"/109 (117, 125.5)cm
- Length 23½ (24, 24½)"/59.5 (61, 62)cm
- Upper arm 19 (20, 21½)"/48 (51, 55)cm

MATERIALS
- 6 3½oz/100g balls (each approx 110yd/100m) of Rowan Yarns *Polar* (wool/alpaca/acrylic⑥) in #643 purple (MC)
- 2 balls each in #649 orange (A) and #641 red (B)
- 1 ball in #644 dk green (C)
- One pair size 11 (8mm) needles or size to obtain gauge
- Size 11 (8mm) circular needle, 16"/40cm long

GAUGE
10 sts and 16 rows to 4"/10cm over St st using size 11 (8mm) needles.
Take time to check gauge.

Note When changing colors, twist yarns on WS to prevent holes in work. Use a separate ball of yarn for each block of color.

BACK
With MC, cast on 54 (58, 62) sts. K 2 rows with MC, k 2 rows with A, k 2 rows with C, k 2 rows with B. Then beg with row 1 for chosen size, work in color pat foll chart through row 88 (90, 92). Piece measures approx 23½ (24, 24½)"/59.5 (61, 62)cm from beg. Bind off.

FRONT
Work as for back through row 80 (82, 84). Piece measures approx 21½ (22, 22½)"/54.5 (56, 57)cm from beg.

Neck shaping
Next row (RS) Work 22 (24, 26) sts, join 2nd balls of yarn and bind off center 10 sts (in corresponding colors), work to end. Working both sides at once, dec 1 st from each neck edge every other row 3 times— 19 (21, 23) sts rem each side. When row 88 (90, 92) of chart is completed, bind off rem sts each side for shoulders.

SLEEVES

With MC, cast on 28 (30, 32) sts. Work 8 rows in garter st as for back. Then cont with MC in St st, inc 1 st each side every 4th row 8 times, every 6th row 2 (2, 3) times—48 (50, 54) sts. Work even until piece measures 13½ (14½, 15½)"/34 (37, 39.5)cm from beg. Bind off.

FINISHING

Block pieces to measurements. Sew one shoulder seam.

Neckband

With MC, pick up and k 48 sts evenly around neck edge. K 2 rows each MC, A and C. K 1 row with B and bind off knitwise with B. Sew other shoulder and neckband seam. Place markers on front and back 9½ (10, 10¾)"/24 (25.5, 27.5)cm down from shoulders. Sew sleeves between markers. Sew side and sleeve seams.

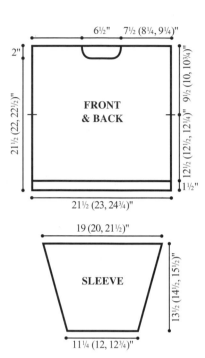

6½" 7½ (8¼, 9¼)"

2"

21½ (22, 22½)"

FRONT & BACK

9½ (10, 10¾)"

12½ (12½, 12¼)"

1½"

21½ (23, 24¾)"

19 (20, 21½)"

SLEEVE

13½ (14½, 15½)"

11¼ (12, 12¾)"

Color Key

■ Purple (MC)

■ Orange (A)

■ Red (B)

■ Dk green (C)

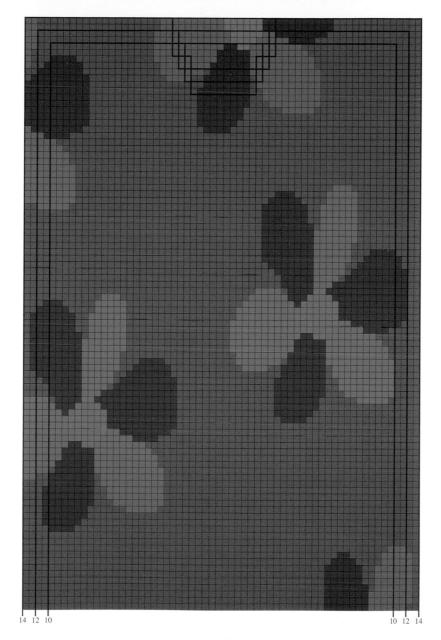

14 12 10   10 12 14

COZY SCARF AND HAT
Wrap star

Layers of scalloped petals don the ends and brim of this wonderfully warm boucle scarf and tie-on hat. Designed by Nicky Epstein.

SIZES
One size fits all.

KNITTED MEASUREMENTS
Scarf
■ 11"/ 27.5 cm wide by 58"/1.45m long
Hat
■ circumference approx 21½"/53.75cm

MATERIALS
Scarf
■ 6 1¾oz/50g balls (each approx 110yds/100m) of K1, C2, LLC *Toison et Soie* (merino/silk④) in #352 salmon
Hat
■ 1 ball in #352 salmon
■ One pair size 7 (4.5mm) needles OR SIZE TO OBTAIN GAUGE.

GAUGE
18 sts and 32 rows to 4"/10cm over garter st using size 7 (4.5mm) needles.
TAKE TIME TO CHECK GAUGE.

SCALLOPS

Full scallop
Cast on 6 sts.
Row I (RS) Knit.
Rows 8 and 11 Knit.

Rows 2-7 Knit, inc 1 st at beg of each row—12 sts.
Row 12 Knit, cut yarn; leave sts on needle.

Right Half Scallop
Cast on 3 sts.
Row I (WS) Knit.
Rows 8 and 12 Knit.
Rows 2-7 Knit, inc 1 st at beg of each WS row—6 sts.
Row 13 Knit, cut yarn; leave sts on needle.

Left Half Scallop
Cast on 3 sts.
Row I (WS) 2 and 9-12 Knit.
Rows 3-8 Knit, inc 1 st at beg of each RS row—6 sts.
Row 13 Knit, cut yarn; leave sts on needle.

Note
Scarf is worked in 2 strips and seamed at center back. Hat is worked flat and seamed. Scallops are worked separately, then joined.

SCARF

Right-hand side
Make 1 right half scallop, 3 full scallops, 1 left half scallop, leaving all sts on needle as scallops are worked—48 sts. K 8 rows (4 ridges)—first layer. On a spare needle, make 4 full scallops—48 sts—second layer. Place second layer on top of first layer; On RS, Join by working k2tog across (1 st from each needle). Cont in garter st until piece measures 12"/30cm above scallops, end with a WS row.

Slit

Next row (RS) K24, join 2nd strand of yarn, k to end. Working each side separately, cont in garter st until slit measures 5"/12.5 cm.

Next row Work across all sts, rejoining two halves. Work even in garter st until piece measures 10"/25cm from slit. Bind off all sts loosely.

Left-hand side

Work as for right-hand side, omitting slit; when piece measures same as right-hand side, bind off all sts loosely.

FINISHING

Weave in ends. Join pieces tog at center back.

HAT

Working as for scarf, make 8 full scallops for first layer, leaving all sts on needle as scallops are worked—96 sts. K 8 rows (4 ridges). Work second layer as 1 right-half scallop, 7 full scallops, 1 left-half scallop—96 sts. Join as for scarf. Cont in garter st until piece measures 6½"/16.5cm above scallops, end with a WS row.

Beg crown shaping

Next row (RS) *K2tog; rep from * to end—48 sts. Rep last row 3 times—6 sts. Slip 2nd, 3rd, 4th and 5th sts over first st. Fasten off.

FINISHING

Sew center back seam. Fold second layer of scallops up toward crown and tack in place. Fold first layer up, leaving 1 down on each side for ear flap and tack in place, (4 in front, 2 in back).

Ties

(make 2) Work 4-st I-cord for 25"/62.5cm. Fasten off. Sew to ends of flaps. Tie a knot at lower end of each cord.

Dress code. Classic wide ribs and a simple striped band are the defining features of this easy-fit weekend pullover, perfect for both girls or boys. Designed by Kristin Spurkland.

SIZES
Instructions are written for boy's or girl's size 10. Changes for sizes 12 and 14 are in parentheses.

KNITTED MEASUREMENTS
- Chest 36 (39½, 43)"/91.5 (100, 109)cm
- Length 22 (23, 24)"/56 (58.5, 61)cm
- Upper arm 17 (18½, 20)"/43 (47, 51)cm

MATERIALS
- 3 (3, 4) 8oz/250g skeins (each approx 110yd/100m) of Wool Pak Yarns NZ/Baabajoes Wool Co. *14 Ply* (wool④) in #37 dk green (A)
- 1 skein each in #30 lt olive (B) and #11 teal (C)
- One pair size 9 (5.5mm) needles or size to obtain gauge
- Size 8 (5mm) circular needle, 16"/40cm long
- Stitch holders

GAUGE
16 sts and 23 rows to 4"/10cm over k5, p2 rib (slightly stretched and blocked) using size 9 (5.5mm) needles.
Take time to check gauge.

BACK
With A, cast on 72 (79, 86) sts.
Row 1 (RS) P2, *k5, p2; rep from * to end.
Row 2 K2, *p5, k2; rep from * to end.
Rep these 2 rows for k5, p2 rib until piece measures 12¾ (13, 13¼)"/32.5 (33, 33.5)cm from beg.

Beg stripe pat
Row 1 (RS) With B, knit.
Row 2 With B, work row 2 of rib pat.
Row 3 With C, knit.
Row 4 With C, work row 2 of rib pat.
Cont with C for 22 rows more.
Next row (RS) With B, knit.
Next row With B, work row 2 of rib pat.
Next row With A, knit. Then cont with A only in rib pat until piece measures 21 (22, 23)"/53.5 (56, 58.5)cm from beg.

Neck and shoulder shaping
Next row (RS) Work 24 (27, 30) sts, join a 2nd ball of yarn and work 24 (25, 26) sts and place on a holder for neck, work to end. Working both sides at once, bind off 3 sts from each neck edge once. Work even until piece measures 22 (23, 24)"/56 (58.5, 61)cm from beg. Sl rem 21 (24, 27) sts to holders each side for shoulders.

FRONT
Work as for back until piece measures 18½ (19½, 20½)"/47 (49.5, 52)cm from beg.

Neck shaping
Next row (RS) Work 31 (34, 37) sts, join a 2nd ball of yarn, work across 10 (11, 12)

sts and place on a holder for neck, work to end. Working both sides at once, bind off 2 sts from each neck edge 3 times, dec 1 st every other row 4 times. Work even until same length as back to shoulders. Place rem 21 (24, 27) sts each side on holders for shoulders.

SLEEVES

With A, cast on 32 sts.
Row 1 (RS) P3, *k5, p2; rep from *, end p1.
Row 2 K3, *p5, k2; rep from *, end k1. Rep these 2 rows for k5, p2 rib, inc 1 st each side every 4th row 18 (21, 24) times—68 (74, 80) sts. Work even until piece measures 16 (17, 18)"/40.5 (43, 45.5)cm from beg. Bind off.

FINISHING

Block pieces to measurements. Using 3-needle bind-off, bind off shoulder sts tog. Place markers 8¾ (9¼, 10)"/22 (23.5, 25.5)cm down from shoulders on front and back. Sew sleeves between markers. Sew side and sleeve seams.

Neckband

With circular needle and A, pick up and k 76 (80, 84) sts evenly around neck edge, including sts from holders. Join and work in rnds of k2, p2 rib for 1"/2.5cm. Bind off in rib.

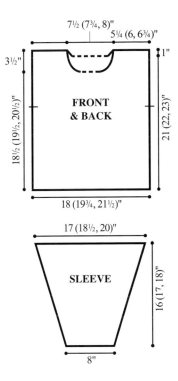

7½ (7¾, 8)"
5¼ (6, 6¾)"
1"
3½"

FRONT
& BACK

18½ (19½, 20½)"
21 (22, 23)"

18 (19¾, 21½)"

17 (18½, 20)"

SLEEVE

16 (17, 18)"

8"

DRAWSTRING LACE CARDIGAN
La belle epoque

Frill seeker! Rows of horizontal lace trim the peplum and bell sleeves of this romantic, feminine cardigan, while vertical lace makes up the body. A pretty drawstring at the waist creates soft gathers. Designed by Shirley Paden.

SIZES

Instructions are written for size 10. Changes for sizes 12 and 14 are in parentheses.

KNITTED MEASUREMENTS

- Bust 32 (36, 38)"/81 (91.5, 96.5)cm
- Length 17 (18, 19)"/43 (45.5, 48)cm
- Upper arm 14 (14¾, 15½)"/35.5 (37.5, 39.5)cm

MATERIALS

- 7 (8, 9) 1¾oz/50g balls (each approx 121yds/110m) of GarnStudio/Aurora Yarns *Cotton Viscose* (cotton/viscose③) in #003 pink
- One pair each sizes 5 and 6 (3.75 and 4mm) needles *or size to obtain gauge*
- Size E/4 (3.5mm) crochet hook
- Four ½"/13mm heart shaped buttons from Lou Lou Button, 69 West 38th St., New York, NY 10018 (212) 398-5498

GAUGES

- 16½ sts and 34 rows to 4"/10cm (blocked) over horizontal lace pat using larger needles.
- 24 sts to 5"/12.5cm and 31 rows to 4"/10cm in vertical lace pat using smaller needles.

Take time to check gauges.

Note Work k1 selvage sts at each end of every row. Selvage sts are not figured into the finished measurements.

HORIZONTAL LACE PATTERN

(multiple of 2 sts)

Rows 1, 2, 3, 4, 6 and 8 Purl.
Rows 5 and 9 K1 (selvage st), *yo, k2tog; rep from *, end k1 (selvage st).
Row 7 K1 (selvage st), *k2tog, yo; rep from *, end k1(selvage st).
Row 10 Purl.
Rep rows 1-10 for horizontal lace pat.

VERTICAL LACE PATTERN

(multiple of 5 sts plus selvage sts)

Row 1 (RS) K1(selvage st),*k3, yo, ssk; rep from *, end k1(selvage st).
Row 2 K1 (selvage st), purl to last st, k1 (selvage st).
Row 3 K1 (selvage st), *k3, k2tog, yo; rep from *, end k1 (selvage st).
Row 4 Rep row 2.
Rep rows 1-4 for vertical lace pat.

BACK

With larger needles, cast on 66 (74, 78) sts.

Beg horizontal lace pat
Work even in horizontal lace pat for 34 rows, end with row 4.

Change to smaller needles. Work 4 rows in St st, inc 12 sts evenly spaced across 3rd row—78 (86, 90) sts.

Next (eyelet) row (RS) K1, *yo, k2tog; rep from *, end k1. Work 5 rows even in St st. P 4 rows.

Beg vertical lace pat

Row 1 (RS) K3 (2, 4), yo, ssk, *k3, yo, ssk; rep from *, end k3 (2, 4). Cont in vertical lace pat until piece measures 9½ (10, 10½)"/24 (25.5, 26.5)cm from beg.

Armhole shaping

Bind off 2 sts at beg of next 2 (4, 4) rows, then dec 1 st each side every other row 5 (5, 6) times—64 (68, 70) sts. Work even until armhole measures 7½ (8, 8½)"/19 (20.5, 21.5)cm from beg. Bind off loosely.

RIGHT FRONT

With larger needles, cast on 34 (38, 40) sts. Work as for back, inc 5 sts evenly across 3rd St st row—39 (43, 45) sts.

Next (eyelet) row (RS) K2, *yo, k2tog; rep from *, end k1. Work 5 rows even in St st. P 4 rows.

Beg vertical lace pat

Row 1 (RS) *K3, yo, ssk; rep from *, end k4 (3, 5). Cont as for back, in pat as established, working armhole shaping at beg of WS rows, until piece meas 10½ (11½, 12½)"/26.5 (29, 32)cm from beg, end with a WS row—32 (34, 35) sts.

Neck shaping

Next row (RS) Dec 1 st, work to end. Cont to dec 1 st at neck edge every other

row 4 times more, then every 4th row 9 times—18 (20, 21) sts. Bind off loosely.

LEFT FRONT

Work to correspond to right front, reversing all shaping.

SLEEVES

With larger needles, cast on 50 (52, 54) sts.

Beg horizontal lace pat

Work in horizontal lace pat for 44 rows, AT SAME TIME, shape lower edge as foll: p2tog 4 times evenly spaced across rows 11, 21, 31 and 41—34 (36, 38) sts. Change to smaller needles. Work 2 rows in St st, inc 9 (9, 10) sts evenly spaced across last row—43 (45, 48) sts.

Beg vertical lace pat

Row 1 (RS) K3 (4, 3), yo, ssk, *k3, yo, ssk; rep from *, end k3 (4, 3). Cont in pat as established, inc 1 st each side every 4t row 8 (9, 7) times, every 6th row 5 (5, 7) times—69 (73, 76) sts. Work even until piece measures 14¾ (15½, 16¼)"/37.5 (39.5, 41.5)cm from beg, end with a WS row.

Cap shaping

[Bind off 2 sts at beg of next 2 rows, 1 st at beg of next 2 rows] 6 (5, 5) times, dec 1 st each side every other row 3 (6, 8) times, bind off 3 sts at beg of next 4 rows. Bind off rem 15 (19, 18) sts.

FINISHING

Block pieces to measurements. Sew shoulder seams. Set in sleeves. Sew side and sleeve seams. With RS facing and crochet hook, work 1 row sc. Ch 1, do not turn. Working from left to right, work 1 row of backward sc along entire front and neck edges, working 4 buttonholes on right front edge as foll: ch 2, skip 2 sc. Work the first one at beg of neck shaping, and the last one at beg of vertical lace pat, (approx 6"/15cm from lower edge), and 2 others spaced evenly between. Sew on buttons opposite buttonholes.

WAIST TIE

Cut a length of yarn 4yd/3.7m long. Make a twisted cord. Make a knot 2"/5cm up from each end and snip ends to form tassels. Thread tie through eyelets at waist.

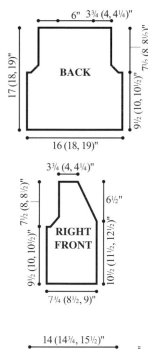

MOHAIR JACKET
Red coat

For Intermediate Knitters

Shape up! This warm brushed coat with seed stitch edges and faux fur trim is perfect for layering on cooler days. Designed by Betsy Westman.

SIZES
Instructions are written for size 10. Changes for sizes 12 and 14 are in parentheses.

KNITTED MEASUREMENTS
- Lower edge 44 (47, 50)"/ 111.5 (119, 127) cm
- Chest 32 (35, 38)"/81.5 (89, 96.5) cm
- Length 29 (30½, 32)"/73.5 (77.5, 81.5) cm
- Upper arm 13 (14, 15)"/33 (35.5, 38) cm

MATERIALS
- 12 (14, 15) 1¾oz/50g balls (each approx 90yd/81m) of Classic Elite Yarns *La Gran* (mohair/wool ⑤) in #6527 red
- 3yd/3m black fake fur trim 2"/5cm wide by Mokuba
- One pair size 9 (5.5 mm) needles *or size to obtain gauge*
- One 1"/2.5cm button

GAUGE
16 sts and 20 rows to 4"/10cm over St st using size 9 (5.5mm) needles.
Take time to check gauge.

SEED STITCH
Row 1 (RS) *K1, p1; rep from * to end.
Row 2 K the purl sts and p the k sts.
Rep row 2 for seed st.

BACK
Cast on 88 (94, 100) sts and work in seed st for 1½"/4cm. Cont in St st, dec 1 st each side every 8th row 12 times–64 (70, 76) sts Work even until piece measures 22 (23, 24)"/56 (58.5, 61)cm from beg.

Armhole shaping
Bind off 4 sts at beg of next 2 rows. Dec 1 st each side every other row 4 times–48 (54, 60) sts. Work even until armhole measures 7 (7½, 8)"/17.5 (19, 20.5)cm. Bind off all sts.

LEFT FRONT
Cast on 42 (45, 48) sts. Work in seed st for 1½"/4cm. Cont in St st, dec 1 st at side edge (beg of RS rows) as on back, AT SAME TIME, when piece measures 21 (22, 23)"/53.5 (56, 58.5)cm from beg, work as foll:

Neck and armhole shaping
Dec 1 st at neck edge (end of RS rows) on next row, then every 4th row 4 (6, 8) times, every 6th row 3 (2, 1) times, AT SAME TIME, when same length as back to armhole, shape armhole at side edge as on back. When same length as back, bind off rem 14 (16, 18) sts for shoulder.

Right Front
Work to correspond to left front, reversing all shaping.

SLEEVES
Cast on 40 (42, 44) sts. Work in seed st for 1½"/4cm. Cont in St st, inc 1 st each side every 8th row 0 (3, 5) times, every 10th

row 6 (4, 3) times–52 (56, 60) sts. Work even until piece measures 14½ (15½, 16½)"/37 (39.5, 42)cm from beg.

Cap shaping

Bind off 4 sts beg of next 2 rows, 2 (3, 3) sts at beg of next 2 rows, dec 1 st each side every other row 9 (10, 11) times, bind off 2 (2, 3) sts at beg of next next 2 rows, 3 sts at beg of next 2 rows. Bind off rem 12 sts.

FINISHING

Block pieces to measurements. Sew shoulder seams. Set in sleeves. Sew side and sleeve seams.

Left front button band and collar

Cast on 6 sts. Work in seed st for 21 (22, 23)"/53.5 (56, 58.5)cm. Inc 1 st at beg of RS rows only every other row 3 (2, 3) times, every 4th row 8 (9, 9) times–17 (17, 18) sts. Work even until piece fits along left front to one half back neck. Bind off. Sew band and collar in place leaving 1"/2.5 cm open at the back neck. Sew buttons on band at 1"/2.5cm below neck shaping.

Right front buttonhole band and collar

Work to correspond to left front button band and collar, reversing shaping and working buttonhole opposite button as foll: work 2 sts, bind off 2 sts, work to end. On next row, cast on 2 sts over bound-off sts. Sew piece to garment leaving 1"/2.5cm open at the back neck. Sew two collar pieces tog. Finish sewing collar to back neck.

Cut and sew fake fur trim around lower edge of body and sleeves.

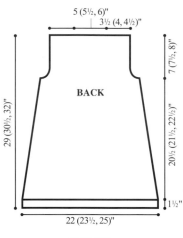

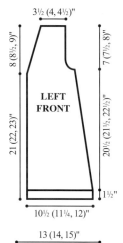

FELTED BAG
Petal pusher

Sassy sack. Knit in a soft blend of wool and mohair, this bag gets even softer when it is felted by washing in soap and hot water. The flower appliqués are knit separately and then sewn on. Designed by Nicky Epstein.

KNITTED MEASUREMENTS

■ 7"/18cm wide x 5½"/14cm tall

MATERIALS

■ 1 4oz/113g skein (each approx 190yd/173m) of Brown Sheep Co. *Lamb's Pride Worsted* (wool/mohair ④) in #105 pink (MC)
■ Small amounts in #28 cranberry (A), #69 moss green (B) and #135 lime (C)
■ One pair size 7 (4.5mm) needles *or size to obtain gauge*
■ Matching sewing thread
■ Piece of buckram cut to fit bottom of bag (optional)

GAUGE

18 sts and 22 rows to 4"/10cm over St st, before felting, using size 7 (4.5mm) needles.
Take time to check gauge.

BAG

With MC, cast on 49 sts for top of bag.
Row 1 (RS) K1, *p1, k1; rep from * to end.
Row 2 K the purl and p the knit sts.
Rep row 2 for seed st for 1"/2.5cm, end with a WS row.

Next row (RS) Work 5 sts in seed st, 39 sts in St st, 5 sts in seed st. Cont as established until piece measures 6"/15cm from beg. K 3 rows (for gusset bottom ridge). Work even as before for 2"/5cm. K 3 rows (for second gusset bottom ridge). Work even as before for 5"/12.5cm from ridge. Then work in seed st on all sts for 1"/2.5cm. Bind off.

STRAPS

(make 2)
With MC, cast on 7 sts. Work in seed st for 17"/43cm. Bind off.

FLOWERS

Make 1 flower with center in A and petals in MC, 1 with center in C and petals in A.

Petals

With MC (A) cast on 68 sts.
Row 1 (RS) Purl.
Row 2 K2, *k1, sl this st back to LH needle, lift the next 8 sts one at a time over this st and off needle, yo twice, k the first st again, k2; rep from * to end.
Row 3 K1, *p2tog, drop 1 yo and [k1 into front and back of rem yo] twice, p1; rep from * to last st, k1.
Rows 4, 5 and 6 Knit.

Center

Row 7 With A (C), k1, [k2tog] 15 times, k1—17 sts.
Row 8 K1, [k2tog] 8 times—9 sts. Cut yarn leaving a 12"/30.5cm end. Thread yarn through rem sts and pull up tightly and secure.

LEAVES

(make 2)

With B, cast on 5 sts.

Row I (RS) K2, yo, k1, yo, k2—7 sts.

Row 2 and all WS rows Purl.

Row 3 K3, yo, k1, yo, k3—9 sts.

Row 5 K4, yo, k1, yo, k4—11 sts.

Row 7 Ssk, k7, k2tog—9 sts.

Row 9 Ssk, k5, k2tog—7 sts.

Row 11 Ssk, k3, k2tog—5 sts.

Row 13 Ssk, k1, k2tog—3 sts.

Row 15 SK2P—1 st. Fasten off.

CORKSCREWS

(Make 1) With C, cast on 12 sts.

Row I Inc 1 st in each st across—24 sts.
Bind off.

(Make 2) With C, cast on 24 sts.

Row I Inc 1 st in each st across—48 sts.
Bind off.

FELTING

Felt all pieces of bag tog at the same time. *Fill a sink with hot water and detergent. Agitate pieces with hands. Transfer pieces to a basin of ice water and agitate again. Rep from * until pieces are fully matted and shrunk to about 1/3 the original size. Squeeze out excess water and lay pieces on a towel to dry.

FINISHING

Fold up bag in half with gusset at bottom and sew sides tog along seed st edges. Sew straps to inside front and back to that approx 1½"/4cm of strap is sewn to inside. Pleat bags at side and sew in place. Sew bag closed at top for complete width of straps to hold straps firmly in place. Foll photo, sew flowers on top of each other and surround by leaves and corkscrews.

Mod squad. Cool geometrics in retro colors combined with chunky boucle yarn make this pullover a big hit. Deep slanted shoulders give a fashionable fit. Designed by Gabrielle Hamill.

SIZES

Instructions are written for size 10. Changes for size 12/14 are in parentheses.

KNITTED MEASUREMENTS

- Lower edge 31 (33)"/78.5 (84)cm
- Chest 35 (37)"/89 (94)cm
- Length 18 (19½)"/45.5 (49.5)cm
- Upper arm 12"/30cm

MATERIALS

- 5 (6) 1¾oz/50g balls (each approx 54yd/50m) of Karabella Yarns *Puffy* (wool⑥) in #51 olive (A)
- 2 balls each in #53 burgundy (B) and #52 rust (C)
- 1 ball in #54 brown (D)
- One pair size 15 (10mm) needles *or size to obtain gauge*

GAUGE

8 sts and 12 rows to 4"/10cm over St st using size 15 (10mm) needles.
Take time to check gauge.

Notes

I Work each block of color with a separate ball of yarn. Do not carry colors across back of work.

2 When working M1 inc's at center of sleeve, the outside stripe in C or B will retain the same number of sts (5 sts) throughout.

BACK

With size 15 (10mm) needles, cast on 10 (11) sts with B, then 21 (22) sts with A for a total of 31 (33) sts. Beg with row 1 of chart for back, work foll chart through row 24.

Row 25 (inc row) K1, inc 1 st in next st, k to last 3 sts, inc 1 st in next st, k2. Rep inc row every 4th row twice, every 6th row once, every 4th row 1 (2) times—41 (45) sts. Work even through row 47 (48).

Shoulder shaping
Bind off 3 sts at beg of next 8 rows, 2 sts at beg of next 0 (2) rows—17 sts. Bind off.

FRONT

Foll chart for front, work as for back.

LEFT SLEEVE

With size 15 (10mm) needles, cast on 11 sts with A, then 5 sts with C for a total of 16 sts. Cont to foll chart through row 6.
Row 7 (inc row) K8, M1, k to end. Cont to inc 1 st at center by M1 every 4th row 7 times more—24 sts. Work even through row 36 (40). Bind off.

FINISHING

Block pieces to measurements. Sew shoulder seams. Place markers at 6"/15cm down from shoulders. Sew sleeves to armholes between markers. Sew side and sleeve seams.

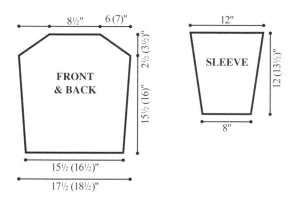

FRONT & BACK

8½"   6 (7)"

2½ (3½)"

15½ (16)"

15½ (16½)"

17½ (18½)"

SLEEVE

12"

12 (13½)"

8"

FRONT

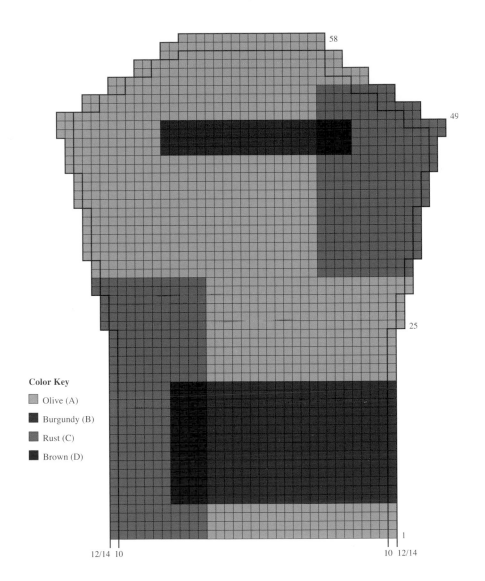

Color Key

▨ Olive (A)

■ Burgundy (B)

■ Rust (C)

■ Brown (D)

58

49

25

1

12/14 10   10 12/14

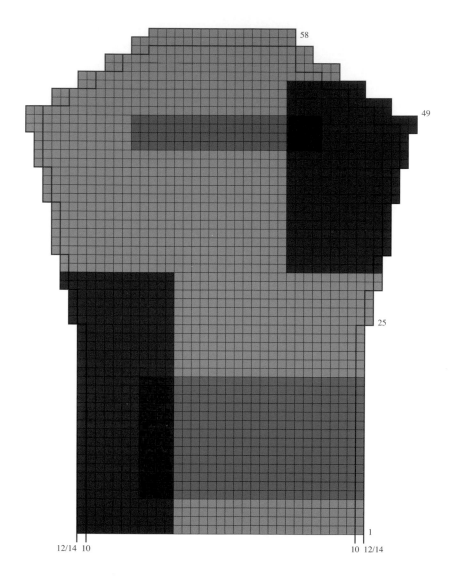

58

49

25

1

12/14 10

10 12/14

LEFT SLEEVE

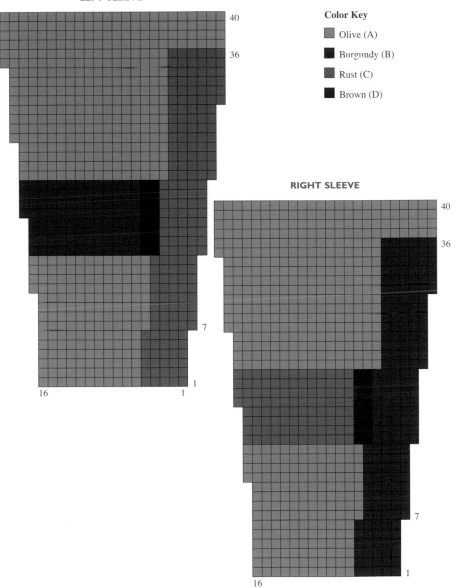

Color Key
- ☐ Olive (A)
- ■ Burgundy (B)
- ■ Rust (C)
- ■ Brown (D)

RIGHT SLEEVE

RESOURCES

Write to the yarn companies listed below for purchasing and mail-order information.

AURORA YARNS
PO Box 3068
Moss Beach, CA 94038

BAABAJOES WOOL COMPANY
PO Box 26064
Lakewood, CO 80226

BERROCO, INC.
PO Box 367
Uxbridge, MA 01569

BROWN SHEEP CO.
100662 County Road 16
Mitchell, NE 69357

CLASSIC ELITE YARNS
300A Jackson Street
Lowell, MA 01852

CLECKHEATON
distributed by
Plymouth Yarn

COATS AND CLARK, INC.
Attn: Consumer Service
PO Box 12229
Greenville, SC 29612-0229

DALE OF NORWAY
N16 W23390 Stoneridge Dr.
Suite A
Waukesha, WI 53188

GARNSTUDIO
distributed by
Aurora Yarns

GGH
distributed by
Muench Yarns

JCA
35 Scales Lane
Townsend, MA 01469

K1C2, LLC
2220 Eastman Ave. #105
Ventura, CA 93003

KARABELLA YARNS
1201 Broadway
New York, NY 10001

LANE BORGOSESIA
PO Box 217
Colorado Springs, CO 80903

LION BRAND YARN CO.
34 West 15th Street
New York, NY 10011

MOKUBA
55 West 39 St.
New York, NY 10018

MUENCH YARNS
285 Bel Marin Keys Blvd.
Unit J
Novato, CA 94949-5724

NATURALLY
distributed by
S. R. Kertzer, Ltd.

PATONS®
PO Box 40
Listowel, ON N4W 3H3
Canada

PLYMOUTH YARN
PO Box 28
Bristol, PA 19007

REYNOLDS
distributed by
JCA

ROWAN YARNS
5 Northern Blvd.
Amherst, NH 03031

S. R. KERTZER, LTD.
105A Winges Road
Woodbridge, ON L4L 6C2
Canada

TRENDSETTER YARNS
16742 Stagg Street
Suite 104
Van Nuys, CA 91406

UNIQUE KOLOURS
1428 Oak Lane
Downingtown, PA 19335

WOOLPAK YARNS NZ
distributed by
Baabajoes Wool Company

*Write to US resources for
mail-order availability
of yarns not listed.*

AURORA YARNS
PO Box 28553
Aurora, ON L4G 6S6

BERROCO, INC.
distributed by
S. R. Kertzer, Ltd.

CLASSIC ELITE YARNS
distributed by
S. R. Kertzer, Ltd.

DIAMOND YARN
9697 St. Laurent
Montreal, PQ H3I 2N1
and
155 Martin Ross, Unit #3
Toronto, ON M3J 2L9

**LES FILS MUENCH,
CANADA**
5640 Rue Valcourt
Brossard, Quebec J4W 1C5

MOKUBA
577 Queen St. W.
Toronto, ON M5V2B6

MUENCH YARNS, INC.
distributed by
Les Fils Muench, Canada

NATURALLY
distributed by
S. R. Kertzer, Ltd.

PATONS ®
PO Box 40
Listowel, ON N4W 3H3

ROWAN
distributed by
Diamond Yarn

S. R. KERTZER, LTD.
105A Winges Rd.
Woodbridge, ON L4L 6C2

UK RESOURCES

*Not all yarns used in this
book are available in
the UK. For yarns not
available, make a
comparable substitute or
contact the US manufacturer
for purchasing and
mail-order information.*

ROWAN YARNS
Green Lane Mill
Holmfirth
West Yorks HD7 1RW
Tel: 01484-681881

SILKSTONE
12 Market Place
Cockermouth
Cumbria, CA13 9NQ
Tel: 01900-821052

**THOMAS RAMSDEN
GROUP**
Netherfield Road
Guiseley
West Yorks LS20 9PD
Tel: 01943-872264

VOGUE KNITTING TEEN KNITS

Editor-in-Chief
TRISHA MALCOLM

Art Director
CHI LING MOY

Executive Editor
CARLA S. SCOTT

Contributing Editor
BETTY CHRISTIANSEN

Instructions Editors
KAREN GREENWALD
CHARLOTTE PARRY
MARI LYNN PATRICK

Schematics
CHARLOTTE PARRY

Knitting Coordinator
JEAN GUIRGUIS

Yarn Coordinator
VERONICA MANNO

Editorial Coordinator
MICHELLE LO

Photography
BOBB CONNORS

Book Manager
THERESA MCKEON

Production Manager
DAVID JOINNIDES
■

President, SOHO Publishing Company
ART JOINNIDES